HIS
LIBRARY

28-7-86

U S S

PEOPLE'S
MON

SINKIANG

AFGHANISTAN

R.Indus

KASHMIR

W. PAKISTAN

TIBET

Karachi

Delhi

Lhasa

NEPAL

R.Ganges

BHUTAN

PAKISTAN

Arabian

Calcutta

Sea

INDIA

BURMA

Bay of
Bengal

Vien

THAIL

Bang

Colombo

CEYLON

INDIAN OCEAN

SUMATRA

M

Asia Today

0   500   1000

MILES

R

LIC OF
IA

or

Harbin

MANCHURIA

Vladivostock

N.

JAPAN

KOREA

Mukden

Peking

Seoul

Tokyo

S.

Yellow River

Sian

INA

Nanking

Shanghai

East China Sea

TROPIC OF CANCER

Chungking

PACIFIC

Canton

FORMOSA

Hong Kong

HAINAN

N.

VIETNAM

South

PHILIPPINE

OCEAN

China

DIA

S.

ISLANDS

Saigon

Sea

EQUATOR

BRUNEI

YSIA

WEST
IRIAN

NEW
GUINEA

RE

KALIMANTAN

SULAWESI

NDONESIA

akarta

JAVA

Darwin

AUSTRALIA

REGMARAD

Modern China

Titles in this series

MODERN TIMES

Modern China

John Robottom
CREWE COLLEGE OF EDUCATION

LONGMAN

LONGMAN GROUP LIMITED
Longman House, Burnt Mill, Harlow,
Essex CM20 2JE, England
and Associated Companies throughout the World.

First published 1967
Nineteenth impression 1986

ISBN 0 582 20433 X

Produced by Longman Group (FE) Ltd
Printed in Hong Kong

Acknowledgements

We are grateful to the author and William Heinemann Ltd. for permission to
include extracts from *Journey to Red China* by R. Payne.

For permission to reproduce photographs we are grateful to the following:
Academia Historica—page 2; Camera Press—cover and page 120; J. Allan Cash—
page 130 top; *Das Studio*, Darjeeling—page 155; Harrison Forman World Travel
Inc.—pages 111 and 112; Keystone Press—page 28; Mansell Collection—pages
40, 41 and 83; Paul Popper—pages 6, 9, 10, 25, 46, 50, 52, 56, 74, 75, 93, 101,
109, 123, 124, 129, 130 bottom, 134, 135, 145, 146, 148, 151, 161, 163 and 165;
Pictorial Press—page 108; Radio Times Hulton Picture Library—pages 7, 13, 15,
21, 24, 30, 33, 58, 63, 85, 94, 98, 100, 105, 140 and 160.
The photograph on page 57 is from F. Krarup-Nielson, *The Dragon Awakes*, by
permission of The Bodley Head Ltd., and that on page 103 is from J. M. Bertram,
Crisis in China, by permission of Macmillan and Co. Ltd.

Those maps which have been redrawn from copyright material are by kind
permission of the following: Basil Blackwell for page 143 from M. N. Duffy,
The Twentieth Century; The Clarendon Press, Oxford for page 133 from Ping
Chia-Kuo, *China*; *The Economist* for page 156; Faber and Faber Ltd. for page 29
from M. Collis, *Foreign Mud*; Penguin Books Ltd. for page 87 from C. P.
Fitzgerald, *The Birth of Communist China*; University Tutorial Press Ltd. for page 19
from W. B. Cornish, *Modern Geography Series, Book 5, 'Asia'*. The maps on pages 29, 34,
42 and 72 have been based on similar ones in Stokes, *The Extreme East* (Longmans)

Preface

More than two hundred years before Christ's birth thousands of men toiled and died in the cold mountains of northern Asia. They left as their monument the Great Wall of China, six thousand miles long. Beyond the wall ranged wild nomadic tribesmen. To the south were the cities and villages of the Chinese Empire, a centre of civilization where strong and orderly government, settled agriculture, literature and science flourished.

Despite periods of unrest and disorder, the Empire lived on for two thousand years, maintaining the longest civilization known to history. It took hundreds of years for some of its achievements, gunpowder, paper-making and printing, to make their way to Europe. The Italian, Marco Polo, who, in the thirteenth century, spent twenty years in China, feared that his countrymen would not believe his tales of the fantastic land where men traded with paper, burned black rock on their hearths and built bridges which would allow eight horsemen to ride abreast. The Emperor, with his fabulous wealth, his army of civil servants and a postal service which extended well beyond the country's borders, must surely, he thought, be the mightiest ruler of the most ordered civilization on earth. In the eighteenth century European sailors brought home priceless objects for rich men's homes: wall-papers, fine woods and lacquers, and delicate porcelain from which the exotic new drink, tea, could be sipped.

But by the middle of the nineteenth century the 'glory that was China' had faded. She had been humiliated and defeated by nations she once thought barbaric. The peasants, who formed the larger part of her population, lived in greater misery that ever in the past. She no longer produced men of talent in science and art. It was then that Sun Yat-sen was born, growing to be ashamed of the depths to which his country had sunk and devoting his life to reviving her fortunes. He died with the task begun, but incomplete, in 1925.

He was followed by two men, Chiang Kai-shek and Mao
Tse-tung, who fought each other for the leadership of the
nation each wanted to make great. This book tells the story of
these three men and of the transformed country that has now
emerged as a new giant on the world's stage.

Contents

Contents

Prologue —
A Narrow Escape

'There is a friend of yours imprisoned in the Chinese legation here, since last Sunday. They intend sending him out to China where it is certain they will hang him. It is very sad for the poor man and unless something is done at once he will be taken away and no one will know it. I dare not sign my name but this is the truth, so believe what I say. Whatever you do must be done at once or it will be too late.'

Dr James Cantlie read this note a few moments after it had been pushed under the door of his London home, late at night on Saturday 17 October 1896. He guessed immediately that the imprisoned friend was Dr Sun Yat-sen, an old medical student of his, who had promised to visit the Cantlies a week before and had never turned up. It was clear that Sun was in some terrible danger and that he must waste no time. He immediately set out for the police station.

But neither at the local station, nor at Scotland Yard, could he convince anyone of the truth of his story. All he could offer as evidence was a hastily scribbled note and, without more proof, no policeman was likely to believe his fantastic tale of a kidnapping in the heart of London.

Next morning he took his story to a judge, hoping for a court order for Sun's release, only to meet a second difficulty. Foreign legations and embassies, the judge pointed out, were regarded as being foreign territory and English laws did not apply there. So, even if a case of illegal arrest had taken place, the courts could do nothing.

Fortunately for Sun, Dr Cantlie did not let the matter rest, and his next move was to make a statement to an official at the Foreign Office. Here the matter was treated more seriously. The British Government would lose face if Sun were smuggled out of the country without its consent. Six detectives were posted outside the legation, for, even if the authorities could

I

Sun Yat-sen

not enter the building, they could prevent Sun being taken through the streets to the docks.

The press, too, learned of Sun's imprisonment and printed reports which were hostile to the Chinese. Finally, on the Thursday evening, the Prime Minister, Lord Salisbury, made an official demand for Sun's release. The Chinese dare not refuse this request from the head of the British Government, and on Friday morning Sun was handed over to a police inspector and a Foreign Office official.

He told reporters how he had met two fellow countrymen, who had asked him to go with them to meet a friend from near his home. Taking him through an unfamiliar street, they had suddenly opened a side door and dragged him inside. He had found himself in the Chinese legation.

Here he had been kept in a locked room, but after a week had persuaded an English servant to carry his appeal for help to Dr Cantlie.

Sun warmly thanked his rescuers for saving him from the horrible fate which awaited him in China:

'First having my ankles crushed in a vice and broken by a hammer, my eyelids cut off, and finally being chopped to small fragments, so that none could claim my mortal remains.'

Why had the Chinese government gone to such lengths to trap Sun Yat-sen? The reason was that he was a professional revolutionary. He had given up his work as a surgeon two years before, and was now the leader of a secret society plotting the overthrow of the Chinese government. His visit to England was part of a tour to raise funds from Chinese living in America and Europe.

How did Sun, a doctor trained to heal and save life, become the leader of a band of men who were prepared to kill and wound their own countrymen? He was certainly not blood-thirsty by nature, nor did he drift casually into plotting and violence. It was his experience of life in nineteenth-century China which made him a rebel.

1 Life in Nineteenth-century China

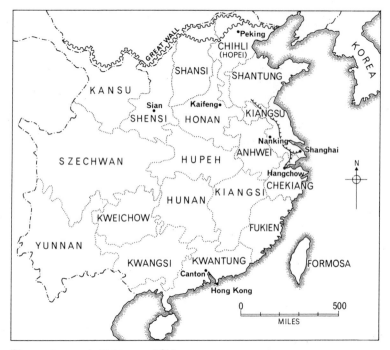

The provinces and chief towns of China

The Peasants

Sun's father was a peasant farmer in the province of Kwantung. He owned a few acres of poor soil in the village of Choyhung, forty miles from Canton.

Even his small property made him wealthier than most peasants, for he lived in a country where the average size of

5

A Chinese peasant of the nineteenth century

farm had shrunk to about half an acre, and where millions of country people had no land and no work. The reason for this was the dramatic rise in population that had taken place since about 1750. Then there had been one hundred million Chinese; by the time of Sun's birth in 1866 the number had risen to four hundred million. In the same period the amount of land available for cultivation had risen by only a sixth.

Farms had been continually subdivided amongst the sons on the death of their owner and the process had left most peasants with holdings too small to provide a living. The shortage of land was made worse by those wealthy landowners who owned more than they needed, and often left large areas uncultivated.

Some of them, on the other hand, rented plots of land to peasants and were harsh landlords. They demanded their rents whether the crops had succeeded or failed, and in bad years tenants were forced to borrow the heavy payments from money-lenders. Many peasants owed the full value of the crops for many years ahead. Sooner or later, they had to surrender their land to the money-lenders and join the starving millions.

From an early age Sun stood in the flooded fields, pushing seedlings, grown in nearby seed-beds, deep into the mud. He learned how to reap the rice, grasping each plant with one hand and cutting it with a knife held in the other. Between the sowing and reaping, there were irrigation channels to dig and their banks to be periodically broken to flood the fields. With friends, he spent countless dreary hours treading the wheel-pump that lifted water to the higher ground. At other times he made long journeys, carrying manure in two baskets slung from a bamboo yoke across his shoulders.

His mother shared in the work, even though her 'lily feet' made it difficult for her to hobble to the fields. 'Lily feet' were an important mark of respectability in China, and all but the poorest families copied the fashion.

From about the age of five, girls had their feet bound tight with strong strips of cotton. Only the big toe remained free.

The results of foot binding. From about six years of age, this Chinese woman's feet had been tightly bound and the four small toes forced under the big toe. Eventually the bones broke and re-set in this position, forcing the arch of the instep upwards

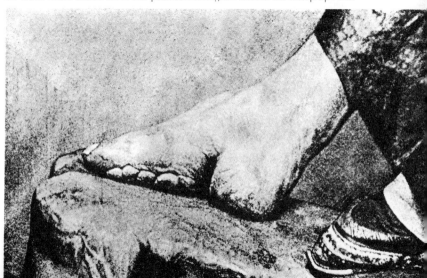

The other four were bent under the foot. The feet remained bound for several years while the bones were gradually broken and the instep was forced into a high arch. During this time the pain was constant and walking was an agony. Sun pleaded with his mother to unbind his sister's feet and relieve her pain. But, like all devoted Chinese mothers, she refused and the binding was only taken off when his sister's deformity had become permanent.

In addition to the rice crop, Sun's father grew sweet potatoes and kept pigs and hens in the yard of his little house. This was a simple building made of a wooden framework, filled in with a mixture of mud, lime and straw. There were two rooms, a kitchen and a living room which served also as a bedroom for the whole family. The family slept on hard wooden beds and Sun soon decided on his favourite pillow:

'I early learned to prefer a pillow made of a bag filled with beans. It was not as uncomfortable as a brick covered with cloth, nor as soft as a pillow of tea-leaves.'

At dawn the family rose to begin the day with a breakfast of boiled rice. The only other meal of the day was at about four o'clock. This was again rice, but usually with the addition of vegetables and, on rare occasions, small pieces of fish or pork.

The Spirits

His father's first task of the day was to carry out the routine that went on daily in millions of homes. He lit a stick of incense at the door, bowed to the north and south, to the east and west and then went into the living room to bow before the family shrine, on which he placed the incense. Above the shrine hung strips of wood inscribed with the names of his ancestors. It was the common belief that the spirits of one's forebears made their home in these ancestral tablets and kept a constant watch over the affairs of the household.

The Chinese believed in the existence of many spirits. They especially respected the Kitchen God, who made his home in a brightly coloured picture hanging over the kitchen stove. Once a year, on New Year's Eve, he left the kitchen to report in heaven on the conduct of the household. The picture was

A man from North China seated in front of his household god. In this region of soft stone, gods were often stored in niches carved in the hillside near the peasant's home

burned, and replaced a few days later.

The air outside was the home of many spirits and great pains had to be taken not to interfere with their flight. Before a new building went up, it was necessary to consult a neighbour skilled in the art of Feng Shui, who would survey the site and advise on its exact height, position and direction. His advice was sought also on the occasion of funerals, so that the grave was dug in the position which would allow the spirit of the dead to escape easily from the body.

Each village possessed a wooden temple. At its doors stood figures of guardian spirits who protected the idols within. Villagers came frequently to burn incense before the shrine of these idols representing the Mother of the Gods, the Earth Goddess and the Northern Emperor.

The Northern Emperor represented the mythical figure who, Sun was taught, had founded the Chinese Empire. There was no such single figure in fact. The Chinese Empire had sprung from the development of small civilized communities which existed on the flood plain of the Yellow River as early as four thousand B.C. These had all been brought together by the

9

Ch'in rulers of the third century B.C., but it was not until several more centuries had passed that the Empire was extended to include the valley of the river Yangtse and the regions of south China.

The early communities had believed that their king was a demi-god, half-god half-man, who returned to live with the gods on his death. This belief had passed into later Empires with the idea that the Emperor's right to rule came from heaven; he had received the 'Mandate of Heaven' as the Chinese put it.

The Rulers

Since the first Emperor, of Ch'in times, there had been about a dozen ruling families or dynasties. All of these 'Sons of Heaven' had been absolute rulers, governing without taking the advice of any form of parliament or council. Their commands were issued as 'decrees of heaven' and it was unthinkable that anyone should disobey a decree, or even question its wisdom.

It was the task of officials, known as mandarins, to see that the emperor's wishes were carried out. There was one in charge of each district and, in addition to enforcing imperial decrees, he also acted as tax collector and was responsible for keeping law and order. In the past, the mandarins had mostly been honest and efficient, but after the beginning of the nineteenth century it was rare to find one who was not thoroughly corrupt.

Almost without exception, they demanded higher taxes

A Mandarin holding court, photographed at Canton about 1900

than were due and pocketed the difference between the amount collected and the sum they forwarded to the Emperor at Peking. It was no use protesting about this, because the mandarins also had the powers of police chief and magistrate. Sun was about ten when three brothers who owned the finest house and farm in his village refused to pay the unjustly high tax which the mandarin demanded. The mandarin promptly arrested them on false charges, had two imprisoned and the third decapitated; he was then able to confiscate their property for his own use.

But this harsh and cruel man took no action against the pirates who had their hideouts in the creeks and streams of the area. Sun once had to stand by and watch helplessly whilst a gang of pirates battered down a neighbour's door, and stole all his property in broad daylight. The mandarin had troops at his disposal, but made no effort tó use them to hunt down the thieves.

Two Thousand Years of Oppression

The life of a Chinese peasant was one of unending poverty and continual oppression by those who ruled over him. To most Chinese, noblemen and peasants alike, this situation seemed part of the natural order of things. The Chinese Empire had grown strong and wealthy as a result of the labour of countless generations of poor farmers.

There were a number of huge cities along the coast and on the banks of the Yangtse, but about ninety per cent of China's population had always lived in the countryside. Emperors usually did little to encourage trade and industry because of their belief that the wealth of the country must stem from its agriculture. They drew the greatest part of their taxes from the peasants and they had, throughout history, not only demanded a high percentage of crops, but also made free use of forced labour.

When the first Emperor built the Great Wall, which defended China from the wild nomadic tribes to the north, he conscripted hundreds of thousands of peasants to work in the cold, mountainous regions through which the two thousand mile wall runs. Those farmers who escaped forced labour were obliged to supply grain to feed the toilers on the wall.

It was the same story when, in the sixth century, the Emperor Yang the Terrible constructed the Grand Canal. This was a magnificent, thousand mile long waterway which connected the capital with the Yangtse river. Its value as a link between north and south China was immense, but so was the cost. Chroniclers described how the Emperor ordered that every fifth family provide a labourer, so that he had five million peasants working under the watchful eye of fifty thousand soldiers. Two million workmen died before the task was completed.

There was military service, too. China's land frontiers are long and run through barren mountainous regions in the north and west, often more than a thousand miles away from the plains and river valleys of the east. Outside the borders lived warlike people, mostly nomadic tribesmen such as the Mongols, and, to keep them out, large forces of frontier guards were needed. A soldiers' song of the ninth century described their feelings:

> Three hundred and sixty thousand men dragged from
> their homes, ·
> Weep as they bid their families farewell.
> Since it is the will of the prince they must obey.
> But who is to cultivate the fields?

It is not surprising, therefore, that the history of China is one of almost continual rebellions. Most of them were small-scale affairs and easily crushed by imperial forces, but on a few occasions the disturbances became more widespread. Secret societies, with exotic names such as the 'Red Eyebrows' or the 'White Lotus', recruited members in village after village until the whole country was aflame. Some rebellions even succeeded in overthrowing a particularly cruel emperor. But it was never long before the mandarins and the great landowners regained the leadership of the country, called in foreign soldiers to crush the peasants, and then chose an emperor who could be relied upon to keep firm control.

The great strength of all the Chinese dynasties was the support they received from the officials and the rich land-owners, whose wealth and position depended on the peasants being kept in submission.

Another safeguard against rebellion was the ignorance of the people of other ways of life and better systems of government.

The Village School

Sun began his education at the village school at Choyhung at the age of six. Like all Chinese village schools it had only one teacher and one classroom, filled with the babble of thirty or forty children of all ages, each repeating his reading lesson to himself.

Reading was the only subject taught; and yet even the

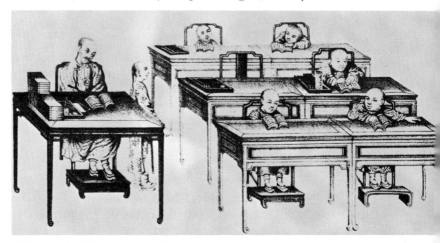

A Chinese school, from a nineteenth century print

oldest pupil was not skilled enough to read more than the simplest books. Chinese is not built up from an alphabet of a mere twenty or thirty letters, as are the other languages of the world. There is a different symbol, or character, for each word and the language contains more than forty thousand characters, each one slightly different in outline from any other. Each has to be memorized by heart, and to learn them all is a lifetime's study. A man considers himself well-educated if he understands five or six thousand and, in Sun's day, very few Chinese could master one thousand.

There was no break from the routine of learning a few new characters each day by repeating them aloud, before copying

13

them into a book with a brush pen. School provided nothing which could excite Sun's imagination. His first reading book, the *Three Character Classic*, began:

> Man is originally
> By nature virtuous,
> Born one family
> Conduct estranges us.

His teacher made no attempt to explain the meaning of the lesson and it never occurred to him that any child might want to understand what he was reading. One day he was surprised to see Sun before him, protesting tearfully: 'I do not understand the *Three Character Classic*. What is the use of learning by heart something which I do not understand?'

A shocked silence fell on the classroom and the teacher was heard scolding Sun for daring to speak out against the wisdom of the ancient philosophers. It was their writings, the Classics, written more than two thousand years ago which Sun had to read, and never before had he met a pupil who questioned them.

Confucius

The most important of the philosophers was Confucius, who lived from 551–479 B.C., when China was still divided into a number of small states each ruled by a different prince. He spent his life teaching men who wanted to make a career serving as a counsellor at the court of one or other of the princes. His teachings were written down by followers and have been accepted ever since by the Chinese as the best guide to right living.

His aim was to teach rules of conduct and he refused to discuss spiritual questions about God, the soul or life after death. A famous passage from one of the Classics reads:

'Confucius said, "We don't yet know how to serve men, how can we know about serving the spirits?" "What about death?" was the next question, and Confucius said, "We don't know yet about life, how can we know about death?"'

He taught that there were laws or patterns fixed in nature and that men should try to harmonize their conduct with these patterns. Examples of a natural pattern were the relation-

Confucius

ship between father and son, or between king and subjects. To have harmony in these relationships, certain kinds of right behaviour were necessary. For example, sons should be obedient to their fathers and people to their kings. It was equally important that fathers should help and care for their sons, and kings should be just and avoid cruelty in dealing with their subjects.

You were reminded of the importance of obeying your father if you addressed him as 'honourable' and called yourself his 'unworthy son'. Elaborate court ceremonies, such as the kow-tow before a ruler, emphasized the wisdom and dignity of the king.

But ceremony, to Confucius, would not by itself lead to good conduct; it was also necessary to be a good man. He described the good man as one who followed the Golden Rule

15

in all his actions: 'Do not do unto others what you do not want others to do unto you'. Unfortunately, certain parts of Confucianism were stressed more than others. The ceremonies became more and more elaborate and more and more meaningless. Obedience was emphasized, but the teaching that the ruler should feel obliged to care for his people was neglected. No wonder it suited the Emperors to have Confucianism as the state religion.

The Examination System

The study of the Classics in schools performed the same purpose of teaching loyalty and obedience. It was held to be the right training for both the sons of peasants and the richer young men who might one day enter the emperor's service.

For centuries the Classics had been the only subject required for the examinations by which mandarins were selected. To pass these examinations was the aim of every ambitious young Chinese, for there were very few other ways of winning wealth and importance. Every year thousands took food, candles and writing equipment into a small cell in one of the great examination halls. There, for several nights and days, they struggled with questions on the Classics. Of those who entered, only the smallest fraction were successful. But those who did receive an appointment as a mandarin were naturally opposed to any change in the educational system.

In earlier times an education of this kind had been found quite suitable. But, in Sun's day, many Chinese thought that pupils ought to be studying subjects such as science, mathematics, modern languages and history which were being taught in the best European schools. The Manchu emperors and their mandarins were firmly opposed to making the change, arguing that it would lead to the spread of dangerous ideas and to criticism of the way China was governed. The mandarins feared that a modernized system of education would lead to the growth of a new class of businessmen, scientists and engineers who would demand a share in their privileges.

So it was only by the luckiest accident that any Chinese boy could ever get to learn of the progress that was being made outside China. Such a piece of good fortune did come

Sun's way, through the help of his brother, Ah Mi.

When Sun was a baby, Ah Mi had emigrated to escape the poverty of his father's home. He had gone to Honolulu, in the Hawaiian islands, and prospered so much that, by the time Sun was twelve, he was the owner of a large farm and general store near Pearl Harbour. To help his family, he wrote suggesting that Sun be sent to join him. His father agreed and, within a few weeks, set off with Sun to walk to Canton, where he could place him on a ship bound for Hawaii.

2   A Rebellious Youth

Five Years in Honolulu

The *S.S. Grannock*, which took Sun to Honolulu, was small for
a passenger boat in the 1870s, and relied on sails to supplement
the power of her steam-driven propeller. But to Sun she was a
mechanical marvel:

'Oh, there was so much! But I think more than the wonder
of the engine, and more than the wonder of the flaming
boilers was just a beam of iron that reached through one side
of the ship to the other to strengthen it. To me it appeared a
most colossal affair, and I remember wondering how with its
great weight, enough men could get hold of it to put it into
its place. The thought flashed through my mind that the same
mechanical genius that had made the great iron girder had
also devised means to handle it mechanically.'

No English or American schoolboy of the time would have
been unfamiliar with steam engines or iron girders. To Sun
they were marvels of human skill; and they also raised a
difficult question. He had been taught that the people outside
the borders of China were uncivilized barbarians. But was
this so?

'I immediately realized that something was wrong with
China for we could not do the things that the foreigners do.
If the foreigners could make and raise into place those massive
girders of solid metal, was it not an indication that they were
superior to us?'

There were few better ways for Sun to find an answer to
this question than to visit the Hawaiian islands.

Discovered by Captain Cook in 1779, they had become
important trading centres and refuelling bases for the ships of
England, France and the United States. Therefore, although
the islands lie in the east, they had been greatly influenced by
men from the Western nations who had come to live and
work there.

In addition to the merchants, bankers and shipping com-

China is a mountainous country with three lowland regions; the North China Plain and the valleys of the Yangtse and the Pearl (or Si-Kiang) Rivers

pany officials there were teachers, lawyers and missionaries. The Hawaiian kings had welcomed them, and had been persuaded to model their government on the more democratic methods of the West.

There were many signs of the advances that had been recently made in Europe and America. Many years later, Sun remembered one in particular:

'The old Honolulu post-office still stands out in my mind very clearly. I looked upon it as a wonder house, for they told me that by merely stamping and addressing a letter and dropping it into a box I could send it back to China as speedily as a ship could go, without having to wait for weeks and even months to find some emigrant to act as a personal messenger.'

At School

Ah Mi paid for him to attend a school run by English missionaries. All the lessons were in English, and for the first few days Sun was able to do no more than look around and observe that boys of his own age could already read with ease.

When he began to learn English he immediately saw why it was so miraculously simple. The discovery that the language was based on only twenty-six characters so thrilled him that he made rapid progress. After a year he was able to join the others in their lessons.

He learned geography and saw a map for the first time. Chinese teachers never taught geography, for it was unnecessary if you believed that China made up the whole civilized world. Sun now found out that there were great continents across the oceans, and their people had the power to travel and bring new ways of life to places like Honolulu.

At home, calculations were made on a notched tally stick. Here he was taught arithmetic, which speedily solved problems far more complicated than simple peasant folk ever dreamed of. Science thrilled him, for he saw that it was the basis of the Westerner's power to make a machine work for him.

But it was history which made the deepest impression. English history books told mainly of the growth of parliamentary government and the way power had been taken away from the kings. They made much of the struggles of parliament against the Stuarts, and the weakening of royal power in favour of the prime minister and his cabinet. Sun learnt that the real power in England now lay with parliament, whose members were chosen by some of their fellow citizens.

He began to make comparisons with China. Charles I's belief in the Divine Right of Kings was hardly different from the Chinese teaching that the Emperor was the Son of Heaven. If the English had executed one king and expelled another, might not the Chinese one day rise up and do the same? The idea was so daring that Sun's conscience was troubled.

The most striking thing about Honolulu was the absence

Chinese beggars at the time of Sun's boyhood

of fear. At home his people went in daily dread of the mandarin. There were poor people in Honolulu, too, but their fate was not in the hands of one man. They ran no risk of unjust arrest like the three brothers in Choyhung. This did not mean that there was no law and order in the islands. Criminals were hunted down efficiently, unlike the river pirates in China.

Sun questioned his teachers about this and learned that, in the West, the duties of the policeman and magistrate were quite different. It was the task of the police to arrest suspected wrongdoers, but the power to punish lay with the magistrate, who had to be convinced that a person was guilty. Policemen and officials could not cheat and ill-treat people, for they, too, were bound to obey the law.

The law was usually accepted, he was told, because it was made after discussion by members of parliament. These men were elected by the people who would have to obey the laws. Gradually the young Chinese peasant boy began to understand the Western idea of democracy and how it led to a freer and happier life than he had known at home.

By the time he had mastered these ideas, Sun was seventeen and no longer the timid lad who had arrived in Honolulu five

21

years before. Ah Mi was horrified to notice how sharply his brother criticized China's backwardness and poverty. Even before Ah Mi's friends, he would pour scorn on Chinese ways and openly praise the West for its learning, its government and its great scientific achievements.

Ah Mi had no time for such matters; the shop and farm left no opportunity for thinking about politics. But he was responsible to his father for Sun and would never be forgiven if his brother returned home with nothing but contempt for his own people. To prevent Sun falling further under the influence of foreign learning he decided to send him home.

The Wasted Year

Sun left with mixed feelings. He knew that life in Choyhung would now seem impossibly dull. There was so much more that he had wanted to learn from the English in Honolulu; after five years he felt that his education was only just beginning. Yet, as the ship neared China, he felt glad to be among his own people again. For one thing, not all the Westerners in the Hawaiian islands had been as kind as his teachers. He had met many who despised the Chinese because they were coloured, and thought them inferior. Their unfriendliness had convinced him that he would never emigrate permanently from China.

Yet he felt that he must, somehow, continue his studies, so that he could show his own people what tremendous advances had been made by countries outside China. They could then perhaps be persuaded to adapt the knowledge to improve their own country; to drive out superstition and ignorance and abolish injustice and cruelty.

His father insisted that he return to live with the family at Choyhung, and it was unthinkable that any Chinese boy would disobey his father's wishes. But he was unhappy there. Work in the fields exercised his body, but there was nothing to occupy his mind.

This made him rather disagreeable and he would spend hours showing off his newly gained knowledge in the tea house. He began to find amusement in teasing the older men about the careful way they obeyed government orders. To a group who had just returned from paying taxes, he gave a lecture on what they should expect from the government:

'Your taxes should show something each year, in schools and bridges and roads. Where does your tax money go? To the Son of Heaven. What does the Son of Heaven do for you in this Choyhung hamlet? Nothing!'

On another occasion he used a story he had read in the Englishman's Bible to gibe at the government. He held up a small coin, a *cash*.

'Who is the ruler of China?' he asked.

'Why, the Son of Heaven.'

'Is the Son of Heaven a Chinese? See on this *cash* the characters are not Chinese they are Manchu. China is not ruled by the Chinese but by the Manchus.'

This was an easy way to embarrass the villagers. They all knew that China had been conquered by the Manchus, from the small kingdom of Manchuria, in 1644. Ever since then Manchu emperors had sat on the throne, and the majority of the mandarins and army commanders had been Manchurian. The pigtail worn by all Chinese was a reminder of the conquest, for it was a Manchurian fashion, unknown in China until the new emperors decreed that it must be copied by all their subjects.

But the men of Choyhung believed that it was better to accept such things. It was not more than twenty years since the great Taiping rebellion against the Manchus had been suppressed. Government spies were still everywhere, listening for rebellious talk such as Sun's. Many began to think that it would be safer for Choyhung if Sun could be sent away.

One afternoon Sun gave them the excuse they needed. He had gathered around him a group of youths and was trying to break down their faith in the spirits. They refused to take him seriously and, in a fury, he strode towards the village temple. He burst in, crying that he would soon show them that the idols were nothing more than wooden figures. Grabbing the finger of one of the idols, he twisted and snapped it off.

That night the village elders met to discuss the outrage. Their decision was soon announced; Sun must leave the village immediately.

His expulsion did not distress him, for it brought what he

The Taiping Rebels terrorized south China from 1850 to 1864. Nearly twenty million lives were lost, and sixty cities destroyed before they were finally suppressed. For a time Major Charles Gordon, shown here, was in command of the imperial armies who were fighting the rebels. He was, as General Gordon, to lose his life in the defence of Khartoum

later called the 'wasted year' to an end. He persuaded his father to allow him to enrol as a student at an English college on the island of Hong Kong. The fees were probably paid by Ah Mi, for his father would not have been able to afford them.

Sun's Marriage

Not long after his arrival in Hong Kong, Sun made a brief return home. His parents were anxious that he should be married to the bride they had selected for him before he left. He was unwilling, but still did not dare disobey his parents on such an important question.

The marriage was arranged and conducted in the traditional way of his people. His parents had used a go-between to approach the parents of the girl they had selected as suitable. Before he approached her parents, this man consulted horoscopes to discover whether the spirits intended the marriage to take place. When he was satisfied, he took the offer of marriage and the two families then signed a contract, consulting neither Sun nor his future wife.

On the wedding day, the bride sat in a red sedan chair and

A bridal chair

was carried to Sun's home in a procession headed by a noisy band. She alighted, her face covered by a red veil, and went with Sun to prostrate herself before his family's ancestral tablets. This action signified that she ceased to belong to her own family and became part of the household of Sun's family. The pair were then given wine in cups tied together with red cord and led into a separate room. Here, the bride's veil was lifted and Sun saw his wife, Lu Szu, for the first time.

What Sun thought at this moment he never told, but it is possible to imagine him feeling deep pity for his unwanted wife. She was a simple peasant girl and accepted the customs of her people without question. Determined to break away altogether from Choyhung, he knew in his heart that he could never share his life with her.

Indeed, within a few days he returned to Hong Kong and was to see his wife only on rare future visits. We know little of her life but it was probably very little different from that of any other Chinese bride.

There was no question of Sun buying a separate house for her; the custom was that a young bride joined her husband's family in his home. Here she had to carry out most of the daily household tasks under the orders of her mother-in-law, who would beat her if she failed to do them to her liking. Life

25

would be one unceasing round of toil and ill-treatment until her own sons were married and she, in turn, could give up work at home and in the fields, and spend her days bullying their wives.

Lu Szu had no desire to break away from the village life she was used to. She found it difficult to understand her educated husband and his Western ways and many years later, in 1915, she agreed to a divorce. Later, Sun was to marry a Chinese lady who had been educated in America and could share his interests.

His marriage made Sun acutely aware of the need to improve the position of Chinese women. He hated the cruelty and unhappiness that resulted from practices like foot-binding and arranged marriages, and lived long enough to see the first signs of a changed attitude.

3 China and the West

The Opening of China

After his wedding, Sun returned to Queen's College. It was not a long journey; forty miles by road to Canton and then a trip down the Pearl River estuary to the island of Hong Kong.

Although so near to the mainland of China, the island was a British colony. Many thousands of Chinese worked there as coolies (porters and labourers), rickshaw-boys, dockers and shopkeepers, but you could not fail to notice the British influences. The streets were lined with the offices of English shipping companies and banks. There were English churches, hospitals, colleges and schools.

Sun quickly found friends among the English teachers, doctors and librarians, who helped and encouraged his studies. But he soon saw that there were other Englishmen who had come there not to help the Chinese, but to make huge profits out of them. Chief amongst these were the opium dealers.

The story really began in the sixteenth century, when the first explorers from Europe reached China in search of new sea routes. They did not behave courteously. Ships forced their way into harbours before seeking permission. Chinese junks sailing to the Pacific islands were plundered. The sailors were rough troublemakers with a bullying manner. The Chinese soon came to despise them and gave them the name of 'ocean devils'.

The Chinese did not want to trade. They could see no value in European goods and wanted no contact with foreigners. For more than two centuries they did everything possible to discourage them. In 1793 George III sent an ambassador to the Emperor to ask for a trading agreement. He was sent home with this message:

'Though you, O King, live far beyond the sea, you have respectfully sent to Us a mission. You beg for one of your people to stay at the Court of Heaven. This cannot be; it is not Our custom. The distinction between Chinese and barbarians is most strict. We need nothing from you; We have all things. We do not value strange or ingenious objects. The manufactures of your country are not the slightest use to Us. It is your duty, King, to obey Our wishes. Everlasting obedience to the Dragon Throne of China will bring peace and riches to your land.'

Englishmen read with indignation of the Chinese Emperor's refusal to accept the English King as his equal, and his unwillingness to allow an ambassador to live in China. It was unbelievable that he should think that there were no goods his country might buy from the world's most prosperous trading nation. They soon found a product which the Chinese people wanted—and were ready to defy their Emperor to obtain.

The Opium War

This was opium, a drug made from the seeds of poppies. Some opium had always been produced in China and addiction was a serious problem. Men smoked a small ball of opium paste in a pipe and were soon in a state of dreamy semi-consciousness, far away from the cares of the world. Great misery resulted, as addicts neglected their families and their work, and often turned to crime for the money to buy opium.

An opium den

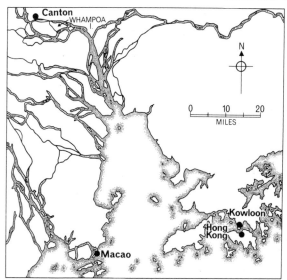

Canton Estuary. The little trade that was allowed into China had to pass through Canton. For a few months each year foreign merchants were allowed the use of a small area in the Canton waterfront, 300 yards by 400 yards. When the trading season ended they retired to Macao

Poppies flourished on the plains of north India, then controlled by the British East India Company, and from 1800 large quantities of opium were shipped to China in English vessels. Near the coast they were loaded on to small boats and smuggled up the creeks and inlets of south China. By 1838 the amount smuggled each year had reached more than forty thousand chests, each weighing $133\frac{1}{3}$ pounds. The Emperor decided to act firmly and sent a senior mandarin, Lin Tse-hsu, to Canton with instructions to end the smuggling.

Lin was an honest official, unlike his predecessors, who had been easily bribed by the smugglers. He believed that the English would give way if he acted firmly enough. Amazed at their tight trousers, he was sure that people who bound their legs with cloth could not fight. At first the British merchants did obey his orders and surrendered all their stocks of opium. Lin had this burnt and the ashes mixed with mud. One workman who tried to make off with a small amount was decapitated on the spot.

Then a quarrel broke out over a Chinese who was killed by a number of British sailors in a drunken brawl. The English refused to hand over the suspected men for trial in China and Lin promptly cut off supplies of food to English ships. In reply to this action, warships entered Canton harbour and sank most of the Chinese war fleet. Thus began the first armed conflict between a Western power and China, the Opium War of 1840–42.

An incident in the Opium War. The steamer *Nemesis* destroying the Chinese fleet of war-junks. In the foreground are boats from other British steamers

The war was confined to the Canton region and was a complete success for Britain, whose army and navy proved much superior in training and equipment. After two years China asked for peace, and the two countries signed the Treaty of Nanking. ,

This laid down that British merchants should be allowed to live and trade in five major ports, Canton, Foochow. Amoy, Ningpo and Shanghai. The Chinese were to pay twelve million dollars compensation for the confiscated opium, and to hand over the island of Hong Kong.

More Concessions

Only two years after the Opium War, America and France demanded the same rights as Britain in the five treaty ports. Britain made no objection because the possibilities for trade seemed almost limitless. In fact she joined with the two powers in forcing the Emperor to grant the important privilege of 'extra-territoriality'.

This meant that the Chinese agreed that foreign citizens should not be bound by Chinese laws but by those of their home country. The reason for this unusual demand was that the Western powers doubted the fairness of the Chinese courts and thought their punishments were too brutal. Nevertheless, it was a great humiliation for China to have people living on her soil whose behaviour she could not control.

The next Western advance was made in 1858, when France and Britain joined to fight the Second Opium War. Troops landed at Tientsin and marched on Peking. They destroyed the Emperor's beautiful Summer Palace before he asked for peace. This time their terms were stiffer.

China had to open more treaty ports to trade and to allow foreign merchant ships to sail on the Yangtse River. Foreigners were to be allowed to travel as they pleased in China and Christian missionaries were given the freedom to preach their faith throughout the country. The news of these concessions aroused the envy of America and Russia, who came forward and demanded equal treatment. The Manchus meekly agreed.

Sun told his student friends that the opening of China to the West was grievously harmful. The foreign merchants brought no real benefits; on the contrary, they brought in unwanted goods and took only cash in return, so that money was flowing out of China in a continuous stream. This led to a steep rise in the price of food and other essentials so that the ordinary people suffered.

Everywhere you looked, said Sun, the wealth of China was falling into the hands of Westerners. Take the railway building that had just begun. Railways were a good and necessary thing and it was due to the backwardness of the government that there had been none for the past fifty years. But these railways were built with money lent by foreign banks and all the profits would leave China. It was the same with the silk factories and the new docks that were appearing in many of the treaty ports.

In a speech made a few years later he explained his feelings in this way:

'We are the poorest and weakest state in the world, occupying the lowest position in international affairs; the rest of the world is the carving knife and the serving dish while we are the fish and the meat.'

Why had China fallen into this lowly position? Sun's answer was the weakness and corruption of the Manchus. The reason for the power of the foreign bankers was obvious, he would explain scornfully. They always took good care to grant whatever loans the Emperor asked for. This had been going on for so long that he was almost completely in their power, and dare not refuse any request for new privileges. He had even appointed an Irishman, Sir Robert Hart, as head of the Customs Service. Hart was able to produce more income for the Emperor's treasury than any mandarin would have done, but it disgusted Sun that such an important post was held by a foreigner.

France and China at War

Not long after Sun's arrival in Hong Kong, war broke out between France and China. The two countries had been on bad terms ever since France had begun the conquest of Indo-China twenty years before. China did not want a strong European nation settled in a land which ran along her borders and, after many quarrels, fighting began in 1884.

Britain allowed Hong Kong to be used by the French as a naval base and, in the harbour, Sun could see the iron-clad French battleships with their powerful guns. In Canton he had often watched the Chinese war fleet; clumsy, flat-bottomed sailing junks that crept about the harbour at a snail's pace. In Hong Kong he saw European troops drilling in their crisp, smart fashion and practising with their quick-firing cannon, loaded with explosive shells. He knew the Chinese army to be a rabble of unwilling conscripts, poorly armed and quite untrained.

Yet, daily, there were reports that the 'ever victorious' Chinese army was winning victory after victory in Indo-

A Chinese soldier of Sun's time. He carried breech loading cartridges which are no use at all for his old-fashioned matchlock rifle

China. This propaganda, deliberately spread by the Manchu government, was readily accepted by his Chinese student friends. But Sun would have none of it.

'Nonsense', he would declare. 'The French have ships of iron whereas we have nothing but clumsy junks of wood. The French have modern cannon with trained experts who know how to direct them, while our guns are barely fit for firing a salute.'

Sun was soon proved right. In August 1885 the scene of the fighting shifted to China itself. A French admiral steamed up the Min River to Foochow. It took him exactly seven minutes to destroy completely the Chinese fleet of eleven huge war junks. Now his friends saw the truth of Sun's arguments and asked what China should do to avoid such defeats.

China would only be victorious, Sun claimed, if she copied foreign methods. To defeat European countries you needed European armaments. You also needed an educated people

33

who understood the need for modern methods. China was trying to fight France when her people were so ignorant that no one even knew where France was. The arguments would

Treaty Ports opened:
——— 1842
——— 1860
- - - - 1876
·········· 1895

Waterways opened to foreign traffic are dotted

Newchwang
Tungchow
KOREA (Japanese)
PORT ARTHUR (Russian)
Chefoo
WEI HAI WEI (British)
KIAOCHOW (German)
Grand Canal
Yellow River
N
Chinkiang
Nanking
Shanghai
Soochow
Wuhu
Hangchow
Ningpo
San-men Bay
Hankow
Ichang
Kiukiang
Wenchow
Shasi
Yangtze River
Chungking
Tanshui
Foochow
FORMOSA (Japanese)
Amoy
Swatow
Tainan
Canton
Si-kiang
HONG KONG (British)
MACAO (Portuguese)
Mengtzu
Lungchow
Pakhoi
KWANGCHOW (French)
Kiungchow
0   300
Miles

By 1900 the Manchus had given foreign merchants the right to live and trade in almost every Chinese port. Their ships could sail on the most important rivers and canals. Important coastal areas had been signed away as leases to foreign governments then turn to why China was so backward. Sun had no doubts at all. For him the fault lay with the Manchu government, which deliberately kept the people in ignorance. They discouraged new learning because it would show the people how weak and corrupt their own government was. To take the lead in modernizing China would be like signing their own death warrant. Rather than do this, the Manchus had meekly given in to every request for land and privileges made by the foreigners.

Preparing for Revolution

The long debates about Western power were a turning point in Sun's life. He now felt that mere education would not be enough to bring about the modernization of China. He convinced himself that the Manchus stood in the way of all progress and that the first step must be revolution against them.

'From 1885, i.e. from the time of our defeat in the war with France, I set before myself the object of the overthrow of the Manchu dynasty and the establishment of a Chinese Republic on its ruins.'

But he was still only nineteen and without any means of earning a living. As a student, he could only expect the support of rather wild young men who would join him simply for excitement. He decided he would spend his next few years training to be a doctor. He could study under Westerners and learn more of their ways. When he had finished he would have the prestige of being one of the very few Western trained doctors in China. People would then surely respect and listen to him.

In 1886 he enrolled at the newly opened Hong Kong medical school, where he was to stay until he qualified in 1892. Here he met Dr Cantlie, the surgeon who gave him most of his training. He thought well of Sun:

'I was most attracted by Sun . . . he at once arrested my attention by his gentleness of character, his earnestness in study and his behaviour as a gentleman in the college and in private life. He was the model and example to the other members of the classes.'

He studied hard, and in the six years won many prizes. But his time was not spent only in study. With three student

35

friends he spent long hours discussing the revolution they felt was bound to come. They dreamed of the day when the Manchus would be overthrown, and argued about what they could do to reform the country when they had power.

'Our thoughts were fixed on the problems of the revolution. We studied chiefly the history of revolutions. When it happened that we came together and did not talk of revolution we were not happy. Thus a few years went by and we received from our friends the nickname of the "four great and inseparable scoundrels".'

No wonder their friends mocked; four young medical students solemnly plotting the downfall of the Manchus, rulers of the world's oldest and largest kingdom! Sun himself must sometimes have wondered whether the fine talk would come to anything. Twenty years were to pass before he could be really sure that the long evenings of discussion and preparation had been worth while.

4 The End of the Manchus

Sun qualified as a doctor in 1892 and two years later he opened two surgeries in the Canton district. They were on either side of the town and, as he travelled between them, he would call in to see friends who had recently opened the office of an Agricultural Association there. It was two years before the police discovered that they were dealing not in foodstuffs but the import of fire-arms.

Sun had added new members to the small group of followers of his student days. They called themselves the 'Dare-to-dies' to show their readiness to give their lives in fighting for a new China.

It was not difficult to smuggle guns into the country; the big problem was money. The Chinese overseas, safe from the watchfulness of government spies, might be persuaded to make donations to the Dare-to-dies. Sun, therefore, went to Hawaii in 1894, and persuaded several wealthy Chinese, including his brother, to contribute. Whilst he was there, a message came from his comrades asking him to return quickly. A suitable moment for action had arrived.

The Sino-Japanese War and the First Failure

By the 1890s Japan was challenging China for the position of the greatest Far Eastern power. For centuries she had been the weaker power. She had also been completely closed to Western influences so that it was as recently as 1853 that American warships had steamed into Yokohama harbour and demanded that the Japanese allow foreign traders to enter the country. Under the threat of bombardment Japan had quickly given in. But, after this first surrender, she took the opposite course to the one chosen by the Manchus.

.She set out to learn the techniques of the West and was so successful that, by the 1890s, she was well on the way to becoming a modern industrial nation. Success made her ambitious to copy the West's military progress as well. Battleships were bought from Britain, the world's leading naval power. The army was trained along the lines laid down by the officers of Bismarck's Prussia. She was well equipped to challenge Chinese leadership in Asia.

The excuse for the assault was to be Korea, a semi-independent kingdom which recognized China as its overlord.[1] After whipping up anti-Chinese feeling in Korea, Japan declared, in 1894, that she would support her in winning full independence from China. This forced the Emperor to declare war. The next few months gave him a sharp shock. The Japanese navy captured Port Arthur and Weiheiwei and completely destroyed the Chinese fleet. At the same time, land forces marched from Korea into Manchuria and threatened Peking from the north. Before they could advance to the capital, China agreed to peace.

The Manchu army was now disorganized and the people muttering angrily about the government's failure to beat off the 'Shrimp People', as they contemptuously called the Japanese. The Dare-to-dies decided on a swift attack on the Yamen, or Headquarters, of the Governor of Kwantung, which was in Canton. Arms were brought in to Canton in packets labelled 'cement' and addressed to the Agricultural Association. They included a few rifles, six hundred revolvers, and scissors to cut off the queues of their supporters once the attack had succeeded.

But while Sun and five others waited in the Canton office, a packet was dropped at the docks and burst open, revealing a consignment of revolvers. Fortunately, a friend rushed to the office with the news and Sun was persuaded to leave while the others set about burning incriminating documents. Before they had finished, troops burst in and arrested them. A few days later they were beheaded, making, Sun said, 'the first sacrifice on the altar of revolution'.

In America and Europe

From then on the revolutionaries were marked men and dare not appear openly in China. Sun fled to Hong Kong to hide

[1] See map of China, Russia and Japan on page 72.

at the Cantlies' home until he could take a boat to Japan. He
also made arrangements for his family to flee to Honolulu, for
he knew that the Manchus would take revenge on them for
their son's activities. The next attempt would have to be prepared outside the country, and Sun decided he must contact
the overseas Chinese in as many different places as possible.
He set off on a tour that, in the next four years, took him
round the world.

He revisited Hawaii and then went on to America, where
he spent six months visiting Chinese immigrants in many
different cities. They were naturally suspicious when he spoke
to them of revolution but, nevertheless, he sailed for Europe
leaving behind several groups of supporters and with some
funds for the next attempt.

His first European destination was London, where his
activities were so nearly brought to an end in the Chinese
Legation. After his rescue he spent nearly three years on the
continent. Here he made friends with socialists who were
building up new political parties to combat the evils which
still existed, despite the progress made in Europe.

Since his Honolulu days he had admired Western democracy and industrial progress. Now he saw that the problem of
poverty had not been solved. He found that millions suffered
unemployment or earned low wages and that they lived in
unhealthy slums in grim cities. He realized that the Chinese
revolution would not be worth while if it allowed similar
conditions to continue in his own country.

The Three Principles of the People

The result of his experience in Europe was his plan for a new
China, *The Three Principles of the People*. The rest of his life was
spent in trying to bring about a revolution which would
firmly establish the principles of Nationalism, Socialism and
Democracy.

Nationalism was the feeling that anything that happened to
China was the concern of each individual Chinese man or
woman. At that time, Sun said, the people of China were like
a 'sheet of loose sand' and lacked the cement of national
feeling which should bind them together. It was the lack of
national pride which had made it possible for the foreigners

The Empress Dowager. She dominated the Emperor and for nearly fifty years was the real ruler of China, resolutely refusing to listen to any proposals for modernization or reform. She died in 1908

to 'open up' China without opposition. One of the first tasks of a truly national government would be to drive out the foreigners from their leases and from their control of Chinese business.

This feeling of nationalism would be greatly strengthened by democracy. It would be some time, Sun thought, before a full parliamentary system, like Britain's, could be introduced. In the early stages there would be a republic whose leaders were chosen by members of the revolutionary party. But, right from the start, the government's decisions must be clearly explained to the people, so that even the humblest peasant would feel he understood his country's problems. Following this period of 'tutelage', or training in democracy, they would be fitted to vote for their own rulers.

The answer to the problem of poverty was the principle of Socialism, or the 'People's Livelihood'. The revolution must be followed by the modernization of industry and transport, together with strong measures to improve the lives of the poor.

After the death of the Empress Dowager in 1908, P'u I, the young boy on the right, became Emperor and his father, Prince Ch'un, acted as regent. P'u I, was captured by the Communists and worked in Peking until his death in October 1967

The aim must be, said Sun, to give 'land to the tiller'. This would mean confiscating landlords' farms and sharing them out amongst poor and landless peasants, so that everyone had the means of providing for himself and his family.

Ten Revolts

Sun returned to the East in 1899. He set up his headquarters in Tokyo and, from there, organized ten attempts at revolution in the next twelve years.

The first was in 1900, when the troops of eight nations were attacking the Manchu armies in north China. They were taking revenge for the encouragement that had been given to a secret society, the Boxers, which carried out murderous attacks on foreign missionaries and ambassadors. Sun made his attack on the south coast, where his chief support lay, and in thirty days the Dare-to-dies had defeated Manchu armies in five places and controlled an area three hundred miles wide.

Ten thousand Chinese offered to join the revolutionary army and waited for the arms that Sun had ready. Unfortunately the Japanese government prevented the despatch of the weapons. All Sun could do was to send orders for the army to scatter before it was caught defenceless.

But the attempt brought Sun's name and his ideas to hundreds of thousands of Chinese. His troops had explained his plans for China in every village they passed through, and large numbers of Chinese had learned to think of Sun as a future leader of the country. An American wrote at the time:

'When I went through southern China in October for the purpose of seeing something of the Rebellion I was perpetually hearing of Sun Yat-sen. He was the organizer, the invisible leader, the strange mysterious personality whose power was working it all. Yet no one could tell his exact whereabouts.'

Sun worked tirelessly to follow up this advantage: writing pamphlets, making speeches, travelling to visit groups of supporters. A second world tour in 1903 brought in more money, and in 1905 he set up a new organization to unite all the different groups who now supported him. This was the League of Sworn Brothers, whose members swore an oath:

'I swear under Heaven that I will do my utmost to work for the overthrow of the Manchu dynasty, the establishment of the republic and the solution of the land question on the

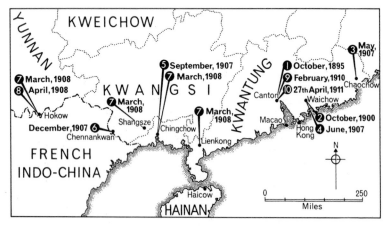

Ten unsuccessful attempts at revolution. The successful 'Double Tenth' took place further north at Wuchang on the Yangtse

basis of a fair redistribution. I solemnly undertake to be faithful to these principles. If I ever betray them I am willing to be punished in the most severe way.'

One of the new Brothers was Huang Hsing,[1] a brave and skilled soldier whom Sun put in charge of the Dare-to-dies on the field of battle.

Sun himself planned and arranged the movement of men and supplies. To do this he took the most amazing risks with his own life. Pretending to be Japanese, he frequently entered China to make contact with the forty or more branches of the League. Once, in Shanghai, he only escaped arrest because of the sympathy of a French official who refused to hand Sun over when soldiers entered his office to arrest him.

He also travelled to Indo-China to plan raids across the long undefended border. Six times he sent forces across to capture a town and hold it for a few weeks. When the Manchu forces arrived his men would retreat, having gained much valuable publicity for the League, and usually bringing with them new recruits. One force that set out with two hundred men came back six hundred strong.

By 1910 Sun was known everywhere in Asia as a dangerous revolutionary, and no country would give him shelter. After making preparations for Huang to carry out raids in south China, he set off on another world tour.

The Double Tenth

In mid-October 1911 Sun was in Columbia, U.S.A. One morning his newspaper carried the headline, 'Wuchang occupied by Revolutionists'. The report explained that on 10 October (the Double Tenth) Huang had seized the local military headquarters at Wuchang. The revolutionaries had then entered the house of a Manchu officer, Colonel Li, where they found the terrified man hiding under his wife's bed. They had dragged him out, promoted him to general and persuaded him to lead a combined army of Manchu deserters and Dare-to-dies.

Within a month, fifteen of China's eighteen provinces were in revolt. The armies of General Li and Huang Hsing had taken all the great cities on the Yangtse and set up a pro-

[1] Pronounced Hoo-ahng Sching.

visional (temporary) government at Nanking. This was to take charge of the country until a new constitution (or rules of government) could be drawn up.

Sun did not return immediately to China. He learned that a group of foreign banks were combining to make a huge loan to the Emperor, which he would use to pay for troops and equipment to put down the revolution. So he travelled first to London, the world's banking centre, and managed to convince the bankers that the Manchus had already lost control of the country and that they would lose their money if the loan went through.

As usual he stayed with the Cantlies. One day a telegram arrived. Sun read it and put it in his pocket. Next day Mrs Cantlie asked him what was in it.

'Didn't I tell you?' said Sun. 'It was asking me to be President of the new Republic!'

On 24 December 1911 the President stepped ashore at Shanghai; a free man in his own country for the first time in sixteen years.

5 Yuan Shi-kai and the War-lords

The Republic at Last

When Sun landed at Shanghai he was met by a group of leading Dare-to-dies, overjoyed with their success. Only three northern provinces were out of their hands and even these were as good as lost to the Emperor. One of his officials, Yuan Shi-kai,[1] had seized them with his private army. Peking lay in one of them, which meant that the Emperor was, in reality, Yuan's prisoner.

The revolutionaries had come to suggest to Sun that they make a deal with Yuan. His army was strong and it would be difficult to defeat it with the amateur Dare-to-die bands; yet, if they could persuade Yuan to join them, he had the power to force the Emperor to abdicate.

Sun did not like the plan. He knew Yuan was a slippery character. Fourteen years before, he had been friendly with a group of officials who had persuaded the Emperor to carry out some important reforms, against the wishes of his powerful mother. At the very moment of success, he had betrayed his friends to the Empress, who had had several of them arrested and executed. His reward from the old lady had been the governorship of Hopei, the province which included Peking. Here he had built up the strongest army in China; but when the Empress had demanded that it take part in the 'Boxer War' of 1901, he had betrayed her and kept his forces away from the fighting. The result of this double betrayal was that he had built himself up into the most powerful figure in China. Now he had the fate of the Manchu Empire in his hands.

Although he would himself have risked a battle with Yuan's forces, Sun reluctantly agreed that it would be more prudent to come to terms with Yuan. He wrote offering to give up the

[1] Pronounced Yoo-ahn She-kie.

45

Yuan Shi-Kai

Presidency to Yuan if he would force the Emperor to abdicate. This he was very ready to do, and on 12 February 1912 China became a republic. The next day Sun gave up the Presidency to Yuan, stating: 'Yuan promises to and will, I believe, support the Republic. He is a man of experience in affairs of state and a loyal supporter of that democracy for which we have so long laboured. I can serve the country as well in administrative work. Let Yuan be President in my stead.'

Why did Sun place so much trust in a man with such a treacherous history? Perhaps he hoped that, as the constitution of the new Republic gave the President so little power, Yuan would have no opportunity for furthering his own ends.

The actual governing of the country was to be by a prime minister and cabinet. They had to work with the approval of the National Assembly, a parliament of elected representatives which made laws and controlled taxation as in western countries. The President was to be merely head of the state, rather like the English king.

Sun disbanded the Dare-to-dies and formed the National People's Party, or Kuomintang,[1] which won nearly all the seats in the first elections to the National Assembly. Sun might have been Prime Minister, but he decided to stay out of politics. What mattered was not his own personal position but the carrying out of the Three Principles. It seemed that the 'People's Nationalism' and the 'People's Democracy' had come about; his task was to work for the 'People's Livelihood'. He wrote: 'Having finished the task of bringing about a political revolution, I am devoting my thought and energies to the reconstruction of the country in its social, industrial and commercial conditions.'

The most pressing need was for an up-to-date transport system, so he took the position of Director-General of Railways and began to plan a system of lines built entirely by Chinese without foreign help. After only a few months he had to abandon this work to take up the political struggle again. This time the enemy was Yuan Shi-kai.

The Dictator

Having been trained as an imperial official, Yuan had no respect for democracy and found it impossible to be satisfied with his position as President. He was used to giving orders; now he was expected to do little more than sign laws passed after long hours of what seemed to him unnecessary debate. He was determined to break from the National Assembly's control and make himself the sole ruler of China.

The first sign of his intention came when he broke his promise to make Nanking the new capital. He preferred Peking, where the army was still under his control and could be used to overawe his opponents. He organized a phony mutiny amongst his men and declared that this meant that he could not leave the north. So the National Assembly was

[1] Pronounced as Kwo min dahng.

forced to join him there.

But the Assembly still controlled taxation and without his own funds he could not be master. The answer lay in the Manchu device of borrowing abroad. He arranged a loan of twenty-five million pounds from foreign bankers, giving in return the right to collect and keep the tax on salt paid by everyone in China. He had no right to make such an arrangement and the bankers were wrong to deal with anyone other than the elected government. Indeed, the President of the United States forbade American bankers to take part in the arrangement, which, he said, amounted to interfering with free government in China. The money was, however, forthcoming from the bankers of France, Germany, Russia, Japan and Britain.

The National Assembly passed resolutions declaring that the loan was unconstitutional, but already they knew that mere words were not going to stop Yuan. A few days earlier the Prime Minister, who had tried to prevent the loan, had been assassinated on Yuan's orders. China was fast returning to the corruption and brutality of Manchu days.

The Second Revolution

Those who had advised Sun to co-operate with Yuan now saw their mistake and looked to Sun to get rid of him. Plans for the 'second revolution' were made openly, because they knew Yuan was unpopular and they hoped for widespread support. Sun even sent a telegram to Yuan: 'You have been a traitor to your country. As I rose against the Manchu Emperor, so, also, shall I rise against you.'

Many old Dare-to-dies rushed to help him, and he led a small army against Yuan's troops. But it was too small and ill-equipped. An attempt to get arms, by a raid on a munitions ship, was foiled when the store-keeper threw his keys overboard. Yuan's troops routed the rebels and Sun fled for his life to Japan.

Yuan was then able to expel all the Kuomintang members from the National Assembly, leaving only a small handful of his own supporters. With no one left to oppose him, he was in exactly the same position as the Manchu Emperors; ruling without any check from a parliament, supported by foreign money and using the same brutality. As he had all the powers of an emperor it is not surprising that Yuan should try to win the the title as well.

A New Empire?

As a first step, he persuaded the obedient rump of the National Assembly to proclaim him President for life and grant him the right to choose his own successor. He then asked for a ballot to find out whether the people wished him to become Emperor. But the only voters were members of the local councils in each province. Each was given a slip of paper on which he had to write either 'assent' or 'disagree'. To help him make up his mind there was a second piece of paper which simply showed the Chinese characters for 'assent'. To strengthen the hint a soldier stood behind each voter muttering, 'Assent, assent'. Not surprisingly, Yuan was able to announce that he would become Emperor on 1 January 1916 and say, 'Such is the will of the people'.

But in the same year, 1915, China was plunged into a crisis which was to end in the ruin of all Yuan's hopes.

The Twenty-one Demands

When the First World War broke out China had declared her neutrality. Japan, on the other hand, had seen an opportunity to strengthen her position in the Far East and declared war on Germany. This gave her the excuse to enter China to seize the German leased territory of Kiachow Bay, claiming that this was done 'with a view to its eventual restoration to China'. After they had defeated the Germans, the Japanese stayed in occupation of Kiachow Bay and the railway, which ran for 250 miles into Shantung province. When she was asked to leave, Japan's reply was the Twenty-one Demands, ominously written on War Office stationery, watermarked with battle-ships and machine guns. They went much further than any demands that had been made on China before. As well as asking for Kiachow and much of Shantung, the Japanese claimed mining and railway rights in the richest parts of China. These rights would have produced more profits for Japan than the whole of the rights owned by other powers put together. But this was not all. China was to agree to lease no

49

The Great Wall

more territory to any power other than Japan and to employ
Japanese financial and military experts to advise her government. China was to become what we would now call a satellite
of Japan.

Yuan was in a most difficult position. He had no forces
strong enough to stand up to the Japanese and, as the British
ambassador said, China 'could not argue with a highwayman
well armed'. He could only wriggle and try to persuade the
Japanese to make some alterations in their demands. They did
agree to postpone the demand that they should advise the
Chinese government, but they insisted on being given the
territories and the mining and railway privileges. On 9 May
1915 Yuan had to sign the agreement handing them over to
Japan.

The news led to violent outbursts of protest. Japanese goods
were boycotted throughout China and demonstrations were
held in every large city. For the first time in Chinese history,
factory workers and coolies took a part. This showed that a
new spirit of nationalism was growing. The sheet of sand that
Sun spoke of was being cemented together as more and more
Chinese joined in to show that they cared about the freedom
and independence of their country.

The demonstrations were aimed not only at Japan. Yuan
was faced with a storm of criticism for not standing up to the

Japanese. It was commonly thought that he had cared more about becoming Emperor than he had about defending China against her enemies.

He realized he must give up his ambition and issued a proclamation saying that China would remain a Republic after all. Within three months he was dead, after a nervous illness brought on by disappointment at his failure.

The War-lords

Yuan's death solved nothing. His short period as dictator had created a state of confusion which lasted for another ten years. In his efforts to establish himself as Emperor, the one group of people that Yuan had never dared to cross were the generals. Without them he would have been powerless. So they had been allowed to do almost as they wished and had been given power in the provinces which was greater than that of the governors. Yuan had granted them so much freedom that gradually their armies became private forces, loyal only to their commander and not at all to the government.

Up to the time of his death the threat of having to meet Yuan's own army had kept these 'war-lords' in check but, after his strong hand was removed, no government could be found which was firm enough to preserve law and order. Yuan's successor was Li, the man Sun's troops had dragged from under his wife's bed. With such feeble leadership in Peking, the war-lords led their bands of soldiers throughout the countryside, terrorizing peasants into supplying them with food and shelter. They swooped on villages without warning, staying long enough to empty the barns of all food and to seize shopkeepers' hard-won savings. They left, taking young men as conscripts and young women as wives and servants for the officers.

The stronger war-lords fought each other for control of Peking and the government of China. But such governments could only last a few months before they were driven out in their turn. With confusion in the capital and chaos in the provinces, it was inevitable that even the poor public services of Manchu times should break down. Irrigation works, roads and bridges fell into disrepair. Famine broke out and millions suffered starvation.

The Kuomintang Government in Canton

It seemed the ruin of all Sun's hopes. The anger which had been sparked off by the Twenty-one Demands, and which had checked Yuan's ambitions, had been damped down by the general mood of despair.

Yet he decided that he must go on with the struggle to set up a government based on the 'Three Principles'. In 1917 he called a meeting of the National Assembly in Canton. Most of the Kuomintang members who had been expelled by Yuan met there and declared that, as they had been wrongfully dismissed, they were still the legal government of China.

Sun was once more elected President of China. But it was impossible to ignore the fact that his government controlled only Canton and a part of Kwantung province. To stay even in this small territory they were forced to rely on a war-lord for protection.

Sun Yat-sen's second marriage. In 1913 Sun married Chingling Soong, the daughter of C. J. Soong, an American educated Chinese businessman. His three daughters, Chingling, Eiling and Mayling, and his son, T. V. Soong, all became important figures in the Chinese Republic. Chingling was much younger than Sun and is still alive today

6 The Rise of the Kuomintang

The May Fourth Movement

The Kuomintang government made many improvements in Canton. Sun's son, named Sun Fo, was Mayor of the City and, under his rule, slums were demolished and replaced by modern buildings, wide roads were built and parks and sports gardens opened to the public.

Sun's own problem was how to extend his government's power from its tiny base to the rest of the country. He had two main opponents: the war-lords and the foreigners. The latter welcomed the absence of a strong government, which meant they could continue their interference in Chinese affairs. They refused to recognize Sun's government because it was nationalist and anti-foreign. They encouraged the war-lords, who were allowed to use foreign-controlled ports as bases. In May 1919, however, the situation changed in Sun's favour when the decisions of the Peace Conference at Versailles became known in China.

At Versailles, near Paris, all the powers involved in the First World War had met to rearrange boundaries and the future ownership of the ex-German lands. The Chinese people had naturally hoped that the other powers would force Japan to give back Kiaochow Bay and Shantung to China. They did not, because in 1917 the anti-German allies, Britain, France and Italy, had promised Japan in a secret treaty that she could keep Shantung. Also, in 1918, the Japanese had made a large loan to the Peking government and, therefore, the Peking representatives at the Peace Conference dare not oppose Japan too strongly.

A storm of anger, even stronger than the protests against the Twenty-one Demands, swept over China, and a nation-wide campaign against Japan was started. A student demonstration in Peking on 4 May 1919 gave the campaign its name of the May Fourth Movement. Several thousand students raided the homes of pro-Japanese members of the government in Peking. Elsewhere, they held demonstrations and protest marches, while shopkeepers and traders organized a boycott of Japanese goods.

Such was the force of the anti-Japanese campaign that the Peking government felt it had to give way. Several ministers were dismissed and the Chinese representatives at Versailles were ordered not to sign the Treaty, though this did not stop Japan keeping Shantung with the agreement of the other powers.

The May Fourth Movement did not die like the campaign against the Twenty-one Demands. It continued to gather strength amongst the millions of young Chinese who were students in universities, colleges and high schools. Countless organizations were set up to work for a better future for China. Young men and women campaigned for an end to superstition and spirit worship, for improvements in the position of women. They demanded that they be taught science and not Confucianism. They became enthusiastic supporters of a simplified language which was easier to learn and understand.

Sun and a few friends had seen the importance of these ideas for thirty years, but the mass of their countrymen had been too sunk in tradition to listen. Now there was a whole generation which had come to believe in them and which knew that widespread changes could not come about until the war-lords were crushed and peace, order and democracy brought to China.

Another important sign of the awakening of China was the growth, from 1919 onwards, of trade unions. Like unions everywhere, they were concerned with improving the pay and conditions of their members. But, as most of their employers were foreign businessmen, they usually became anti-foreign and sympathetic to the nationalistic ideas of Sun. They became an important force in the struggle against foreign influence and many strikes against foreign employers took place. Once, the Seamen's Union in Canton struck and succeeded in bringing nearly all the foreign shipping to a standstill. When Britain, whose ships were most affected, refused to recognize the Union's claims, all the Chinese servants working for British people in Hong Kong came out on strike in sympathy and the shipowners were forced to give in.

As support for his ideas grew, Sun began to talk of a Northern Expedition, a military campaign which should strike out from Canton, defeat the war-lords one by one and reunite the country. But he needed a properly trained and equipped army. To get this he turned to his government's only friend outside China—the communist Soviet Russia.

Sun and Russia

In October 1917 the Russian Communists had overthrown the Tsar, but part of his army had refused to recognize the new government. A deadly struggle broke out between the communist Red Army and their opponents, the Whites, who were helped by the armies of foreign powers. Three of them, Britain, France and Japan, were the same powers that Sun held responsible for China's troubles.

He therefore sympathized with the struggles of Lenin, the Communist leader, and, in 1918, sent him a telegram of good wishes. Lenin, for his part, desperately needed friends for the Communist government. He naturally turned to China, which suffered from what he called 'imperialism'—or interference by powerful modern nations in the affairs of a poorer country. In 1919 the Soviet government officially offered friendship to China:

'If the people of China wish to become free, like the Russian people, and be spared the lot prepared for them by the allies at Versailles . . . let it be understood that its only allies and brothers in its struggle for national freedom are the Russian workers and peasants and their Red Army.'

As proof of their good wishes they said that they would return all the lands and privileges that Tsarist Russia had seized from China.

These friendly actions were followed by visits from communist agents. They found a handful of Chinese who were sympathetic to communism and helped them to found the Chinese Communist Party, which in 1922 had no more than three hundred members. They also visited Sun and suggested that Russia should help the Kuomintang regain

Lenin addressing a meeting in Moscow. On the right, in uniform, stands Trotsky, who played a large part in inspiring the Red Army to defeat the Whites

full power in China.

At first Sun was wary, fearing that he would be accused of betraying his own 'Three Principles' in favour of communism, which was not a democratic faith and whose followers believed, not in giving 'land to the tiller', but in taking all land and property into state ownership.

But circumstances made him change his mind. In late 1922, the war-lord who had given him protection in Canton suddenly betrayed him and sent armed men to assassinate him in his home. He had a narrow escape, with the aid of a young friend, Chiang Kai-shek,[1] and fled to Shanghai.

This forced him to look for help from any quarter and he agreed to meet another Russian envoy, Joffe. He signed an agreement with Joffe for co-operation between Russia and the Kuomintang Party, but he made it perfectly clear that the Three Principles, and not communism, were his goal.

[1] Pronounced Ji-ahng Gai-shek.

56

The Reorganized Kuomintang

As a result of the agreement, young Kuomintang members
were sent to Moscow for military training. One of these was
Chiang Kai-shek, who returned to set up the Kuomintang's
own military academy at Whampoa, near Canton. Four to
five hundred officers were trained there every year and soon
a military force capable of standing up to the war-lords was
in sight. The Russians helped with money and military
equipment.

They sent an experienced political agent, Borodin, to
advise Sun on organizing the Kuomintang. Borodin's real
name was Michael Grusenberg. He had been born in Russia
but had emigrated to America with his parents. For a while
he had been the owner of a school for businessmen in Chicago
and had then turned communist. He had been sent to build
up new communist parties in Mexico and Turkey and was an
old hand at political organization.

Borodin suggested to Sun that the Kuomintang should
copy the Communist Party organization, which was based on
party cells. The cell was a small local group, one for each
street or each section of a factory. Its members were expected
to study the policies decided by the party's leaders and explain
them to the people of their locality. They should also report

Borodin in Canton

on the problems and grievances of the people, so that the leaders could work out the policies most likely to win support.

'All policies and plans of the Party must go through cells before they can materialize. The cell is the Party's ears, eyes, arms and legs among the masses. The Party must have cell organization before it can understand the demands of the masses and the masses can recognize the guidance of the Party.'

Borodin suggested to Sun that the Kuomintang wasted too much time on debate and that the members ought to give up their right to discuss policies. Instead a small committee headed by Sun should make the decisions.

A Conference of the Kuomintang was held in 1924 and agreed to all these changes. Some of the members were reluctant to give so much power to their leaders, but Sun persuaded them that it was necessary for a time 'to sacrifice their individual freedom and put all their ability at the disposal of the party'. They also agreed that the Chinese communists should be allowed to join the Kuomintang. Sun promised that 'if the Communists betray the Kuomintang I will be the first to propose their expulsion'. Although they agreed to copy the communist methods, the conference made it quite clear that the Kuomintang Party still stood for the Three Principles and not for communism.

Very soon after the conference the Russian help began to show results. The cell system began to work and Kuomintang propaganda was preparing the people to support Sun when

The result of Russian help. Sun and his wife photographed with officers trained at the Whampoa Military Academy

he struck against the war-lords. He planned to begin his Northern Expedition in 1925, using the troops that had been trained and equipped with Russian help. He was more confident of success than ever before.

But the Northern Expedition had to wait another year for, at the very brink of success, Sun was struck by an incurable disease.

He knew that he had but a few months to live, and spent the time planning for the Kuomintang to continue the work he had started.

He wrote to Joseph Stalin, who had succeeded Lenin as the leader of Soviet Russia:

'At this moment when I am suffering from an incurable illness, my heart turns to you, to my party and to the future of my country. You are the leaders of a great free union of republics. . . . People suffering under the yoke of imperialism will rely on it for the protection of their freedom. . . . I have ordered the Kuomintang to co-operate with you.'

Stalin sent a reply assuring Sun that he would continue to help the Kuomintang.

To the people of China Sun left a message in his will: 'For forty years I have devoted myself to the cause of the National Revolution, the object of which is to raise China to a position of independence and equality. . . . Let all our comrades follow my writings and continue to make every effort to carry them into effect.'

The next day the man they came to call 'The Father of the Republic' was dead.

7 Chiang Kai-shek

The Officer Cadet

Chiang Kai-shek was born in 1887 into a well-to-do land-owning family in the village of Military Ridge, about a hundred miles south of Shanghai. He did not have to work in the fields, nor struggle to learn to read in a room full of babbling children. He was taught the Classics in his own home by a private tutor.

He was only eight when his father died and he became head of the family, a heavy responsibility. When he was seventeen a peasant in the village failed to pay his taxes and ran away. The mandarin ordered that the rest of the village should pay instead and tried to squeeze an excessive amount out of Chiang's mother. When Chiang protested, he was arrested and, to prevent his being sent to prison, his mother had to pay.

This incident made him want a career which would take him far away from the village. He decided to go to Japan to train as an army officer at the Tokyo Military Academy. When his mother tried to persuade him not to go, he cut off his queue. Fearing for his safety if he went on defying the Manchu regulations, she reluctantly agreed to his plan.

The Japanese would accept only men who had first trained in China, but it was almost impossible to get into a Chinese military academy without influence. In 1905 there were sixty places available and forty-six of these had been filled already by young men who were friends and relatives of government officials. A thousand candidates competed in the examination for the remaining fourteen. Nevertheless, after months of hard study, Chiang was successful.

He then spent two years training under Manchurian instructors. Most of the cadets were Manchurian too, and they despised Chiang, a member of the conquered Chinese race. Their haughty manners and their mockery of his short hair hurt him deeply, but made him more determined to show that he was a better soldier than they were. He did so well that his instructors could not deny that he was suitable for training in Japan.

In 1907 Tokyo was the headquarters of Sun Yat-sen and the Dare-to-dies. Chiang's hatred of the Manchurians, and his bitter experience of the injustice of their mandarins, led him to the revolutionaries. He was a valuable recruit, for he frequently visited his mother and thus had a perfect alibi for travelling through Shanghai, where he passed on messages to the Dare-to-dies.

The Revolutionary

In October 1911 he was on an exercise with the Japanese army when a telegram arrived. Without revealing its contents, he asked for leave and left camp that night to play his part in the Double Tenth.

Back in China, he was given the task of winning over his own province, Chekiang. He went secretly to the capital, Hangchow, and persuaded the soldiers of the Manchu army there to promise to join him as soon as the governor was arrested. He then led an attack of a hundred Dare-to-dies on the governor's headquarters. The attack was successful, the army deserted to Chiang and another province had been won.

After the revolution he returned to Japan and his military studies. With increasing anger he read reports of Yuan's destruction of the democratic Republic. When Sun began the second revolution, Chiang joined him and became his Chief of Staff. After their defeat he and Sun returned to Japan together.

Chiang did not return to the Japanese army again, but remained with Sun, watching for further chances to upset Yuan's power. Several times he slipped secretly into China to organize brief rebellions, but they all failed.

When Sun set up his Kuomintang government in Canton in 1917, Chiang joined him there as a military adviser. He found his work difficult, for he distrusted the war-lord, Chen Chiung-ming, who was supposed to protect Canton, and frequently disagreed with him. After one quarrel with Chen, he left Canton and went to Shanghai to work as a stockbroker. Here he made a fortune selling stocks and shares and made many friends amongst rich businessmen who became important to him in later years. He also made contact with some of the leaders of the waterside gangs that were a menace to law

Chiang Kai-shek

and order in Shanghai. They, too, were to be useful to him in the future.

Returning to Canton in 1921, he found Chen was still in power and wrote to warn Sun of danger: 'If you hope for him to take orders at the critical moment and to respect the party enough to defend it against its foe you will find he is not the man.'

Sun ignored the warning and Chen was able to go ahead with a plot to capture him and take over the government of Canton himself. In 1922 he struck. His troops occupied the city and attacked Sun's house. Chiang saved Sun's life by smuggling him through the streets to a gunboat he had commandeered. For fifty-six days they stayed aboard, well away from the shore, and then decided that it was impossible to regain Canton at the moment. So they sailed on to Shanghai, where Sun made his important agreement with the Russians.

The rescue of Sun was a turning point in Chiang's career. Sun now looked upon him as the most trustworthy of his followers; the only one who would serve the Kuomintang rather than his own private interests. He gave Chiang the task of setting up the new military training school at Whampoa.

Chiang first visited Moscow to study the Russians' training methods. He found it difficult to like the Communist leaders, who, he suspected, were only helping Sun for their own ends. Nevertheless, he used many Russian ideas at Whampoa, and the training school was a great success.

Nearly all the best Kuomintang officers were trained there by Chiang and learned to respect his efficiency as a soldier. His position in the Kuomintang grew so powerful that, after Sun's death, he appeared the natural choice for the leadership of the party.

8 Mao Tse-tung

Boyhood

Mao Tse-tung[1] was born in 1893, six years after Chiang. He had a hard boyhood. His father was a man made harsh and stern by a lifetime of struggle. As a young man he had been forced to give up his farm and flee into the army because of heavy debts. Later he returned to his village in Hunan province, determined to do better. Beginning as a dealer in pigs and rice, he had soon saved enough to buy a farm of two and a half acres. Living in the simplest way possible, he managed to save a third of his rice crop for the market. From his profits he lent money at high rates of interest and soon became one of the richest peasants in the village.

Unless the family continued to work hard and eat little, all the hard-won savings could be wiped out in one year of drought or famine. So Mao, like any other peasant boy, had to work long hours in the fields. At seven he began school, where he showed himself to be a quick scholar. Like Sun Yat-sen, thirty years before, he found the Classics dull and meaningless, but he came across other books which thrilled him. After school, he would creep away from his overcrowded little home to some quiet corner in the fields where he could read, undisturbed, tales of the lives of humble Chinese people and their struggles against hard times and harsh rulers.

This displeased his father, who wanted his help, and there were many quarrels. Once, Mao was so angry at being scolded for idleness in front of his father's friends that he bolted out of the house, swearing that he would leave home. His mother, however, persuaded him to return.

As Mao grew older there were new causes of bitterness. The years 1906 and 1910 brought famine, the first from flood and the second from drought. Famine led to riots and riots to the arrest and execution of several starving peasants. His father

[1] Pronounced Mow Tzuh-doong.

took the side of the mandarins; Mao openly sympathized with the peasants. Worse still was the time when rain fell unexpectedly on harvested rice lying in the open to dry. The villagers rushed to bring it in and Mao's father was furious to find that his son was not at his side. That evening he learned that Mao had been helping poorer peasants who, he thought, needed his help more than his own family.

The quarrels came to an end only when Mao succeeded in persuading his father to let him leave home and attend school fifty miles away.

At School and College

He stayed there only a year, just long enough for his teachers to realize he was a clever boy with a gift for writing essays and poetry. His chief love was still reading. Many years later a friend remembered him as he was at this time:

'When he was sixteen and I was twelve, I met him for the first time. He was hurrying down a road with a parcel of books under his arm. I had seen him before—he always had books. A few days later I lent him a book about the great heroes of the world. It was a book with articles about Peter the Great, Washington, Lincoln, Rousseau, Montesquieu, and Napoleon, and perhaps twenty others. He read the whole book in one night and gave it back to me, saying "We need great people like these in China".'

In the summer of 1911 Mao went on to a High School in Changsha, the capital of Hunan. Here, at eighteen, he saw his first newspaper. It was the *People's Strength* published by the Dare-to-dies. After reading it, he wrote an essay in favour of a republic, which he pinned to the school notice-board. He publicly cut off his pig-tail and persuaded ten fellow students to do the same.

Normally such an action would have led to serious trouble, but Mao's own small rebellion was soon swamped by the news of the Double Tenth. Within twelve days the revolution had spread to Changsha, and Mao watched the battle in which the Dare-to-dies and some mutinied troops speedily defeated the Emperor's forces.

He left school and joined the revolutionary army as a private. He never saw action, but spent his time doing odd jobs around camp. Most of his pay of fourteen shillings a month he spent on newspapers and, from them, followed the events of 1911 and 1912 which led to Yuan Shi-kai becoming President.

At this point he thought the revolution was over and left the army. He tried several jobs, but none were to his liking. So, for the next few months, he lived on bread and water and spent his days reading in Changsha library. It was to him, he said, 'like a vegetable garden to an ox': he devoured almost every book that came to hand, especially western works on politics and economics. Then, in 1913, he enrolled for a five-year course at a Teachers' Training College in Changsha.

As Sun Yat-sen had done at the Medical School, so Mao studied hard but gave even more time to thinking about his country's problems. Like many other students who had hoped for great things from the 1911 Revolution, he was appalled by the evils of Yuan's dictatorship and the confusion the war-lords brought to China. The future of the country, he felt, rested in the hands of the young men and women who shared this disgust with the way things had turned out. But how could he prepare for the future?

One way was to be sure that he was strong enough for whatever trials lay ahead. He led an extremely tough life, eating one meal a day, sleeping in the open and swimming in icy rivers in winter. With close friends he went for long walks. On one occasion he and another young man walked across the whole of Hunan, without a penny in their pockets.

Another way was to create a group of like-minded people. Under the name of 'Mr Twenty-eight strokes', he advertised, asking to meet other young people who were 'prepared to work and make sacrifices for their country's future'. Out of this arose the Changsha 'New Citizens Society', which held weekly meetings to discuss the state of China and study foreign books.

The May Fourth Movement

When Mao left College he travelled to Peking to work as an assistant in the university library. Still desperately poor, he shared one room and a bed with seven friends, who owned one overcoat between them. This was an important time in his

Mao Tse-tung

life, for he made friends among the university professors and
students who became leaders of the May Fourth Movement.

The May Fourth demonstrations began two months after
Mao had returned to Changsha to work as a teacher. He, and
the New Citizens Society, acted swiftly in support of his
Peking friends. The students in Changsha and other towns in
Hunan were formed into a union, and Mao led them in a
strike to protest against the loss of Shantung to Japan.

It was the first time he had organized a political campaign
but from then on he never ceased to be in the forefront of
activities in Changsha. He edited several newspapers, which
were closed down in turn by the war-lord controlling Hunan.
A friend described the heavy strain he put himself under: 'He
often worked for the paper into the small hours of the morning
and then, after a short nap, went straight to his class un-
washed and unbreakfasted.'

But was he getting anywhere? It was in 1920 that he first
began to feel that political speeches and newspaper articles
were a waste of time and effort. His letters of the time show
that his thoughts were turning towards communism.

Marxism and Communism

Mao had for some time been studying the ideas of Karl Marx,
the German revolutionary on whose writings communism
was based. Marx taught that modern society was divided into

68

two main classes, the *bourgeoisie* and the *proletariat*. The *bourgeoisie* were the owners of business and land, who used their wealth to control the lives of the wage-earners or *proletariat*.

He believed that different classes never came together willingly, and wrote that, 'The history of all hitherto existing society is the history of class struggle'. For the workers to improve their position they must engage in war with the bourgeois class. This class war would mean revolution against the state, for the *bourgeoisie* was not only the owning class but also the ruling class. They controlled parliament, the armed forces, education and the newspapers.

A Communist Party member believed that the revolution was bound to come, for, as the world became more industrialized, the condition of the proletariat would worsen until it became unbearable. His job was to work among the proletariat to turn it into a revolutionary force, ready to seize power when the time was ripe.

Most Communists looked to Russia for guidance in building a Communist Party, for Russia was then the only country with a Communist government. It was also the headquarters of the Communist International, which sent its 'Comintern' agents all over the world to advise on revolutionary organization.

The Beginnings of the Chinese Communist Party

At the end of 1920 Mao wrote to a friend that the May Fourth Movement, which tried to educate the people by peaceful means, was bound to be a failure. The letter went on to say that:

'Education in his view needed money, qualified personnel, and schools, all of which were controlled by the ruling class. Newspapers, too, were in their hands. They dominated the parliament and government, made the law, owned banks and factories, and had the army and police on their side. They used all these to fight against workers and peasants.'[1]

So, Mao set about organizing a branch of the Communist Party in Changsha. In the same year a few friends from the May Fourth Movement, with help from two Comintern

[1] This account of Mao's letter is given in *Mao and the Chinese Revolution* by Jerome Ch'en (O.U.P., 1965).

agents, set up branches in Peking and Shanghai.

In the summer of 1921 Mao travelled to the first Congress of the Chinese Communist Party, held in secret in a girls' school in Shanghai. There were twelve delegates, representing only fifty-seven members, but they resolved to go on building up the Party, especially among workers in industry.

Mao returned to Hunan province and began to work among the miners and railwaymen. After winning their confidence, he persuaded them to strike for an improvement in their miserable wages. The employers called in troops, who fired on them, killing six and wounding seventy. This only increased their determination and eventually the employers raised their wages.

Not long after this successful start as a communist organizer, Mao was called to Shanghai.

The Communists and the Kuomintang

While he was in Shanghai, the Chinese Communist Party took the important decision to join with Sun Yat-sen's Kuomintang. They had always looked on the Kuomintang as a *bourgeois* not a *proletarian* party and had wanted to keep separate from it, but the Party secretary, who had recently been to Moscow, urged them to follow Lenin's advice to co-operate with the Kuomintang, to drive out the war-lords and unite the country. Then would be the time for 'the bourgeois republic to be overthrown and replaced by the dictatorship of the proletariat'.

Mao, like his comrades, therefore joined the Kuomintang. His experience as an organizer and writer made him a useful member and in 1925, shortly after the death of Sun, he was called to Canton and put in charge of the Kuomintang propaganda department.

Thus, Mao, the experienced communist organizer, and Chiang, the soldier, were both in Canton at the time when the Kuomintang was about to launch its expedition against the war-lords.

9 The Kuomintang Defeats the War-lords and the Communists

The Northern Expedition

When Sun died in 1925 he left the Kuomintang divided into three groups. On the one hand were the Communists, who had now joined the Kuomintang and were growing in strength and numbers. Borodin, the Comintern agent, had become an important figure in the Kuomintang. At the opposite extreme, stood the Right Kuomintang; a group made up of wealthy businessmen and landlords. They had joined the party because they wanted efficiency and order in China, not because they accepted Sun's socialist ideas. They had been against admitting Communists into the Kuomintang, and many would rather have made a deal with the war-lords than fight them with communist help.

In between was the Left Kuomintang, whose members were not communist but welcomed Russian help. Believing that the most important task was the ending of mass poverty, the Left were closest to Sun's ideas. Indeed, Madame Sun and Sun Fo, his widow and son, were important members of the group.

Chiang Kai-shek, now a wealthy man, was most sympathetic to the Right but, at this time, he supported the Left. He distrusted the Communists and dismissed all communist officers from the army, yet he was forced to agree with the Left's view that Russian help was essential in the fight against the war-lords.

His reputation as a soldier and friend of Sun Yat-sen led to his appointment as commander-in-chief of the Northern Expedition. He was a ruthless leader and gave orders that any officer who led his men in retreat would be shot. The first stage of the campaign was to be a march to drive the war-lords from the cities of the Yangtse valley. In late 1926 the Kuomintang armies set out on their great adventure.

With the army travelled the political agents of the Kuomin-tang, whose task it would be to explain the purpose of the

China, Russia and Japan

Expedition to the people of the towns and villages through which it passed. The leader of the Political Department was now Mao Tse-tung and most of his agents were also Communists.

The agents encouraged the peasants to turn on all landlords, not just those in league with a war-lord. They taught villagers to set up Peasant Associations, which seized the lands of the rich and shared them out amongst landless peasants. In the towns they worked through the trade unions. As the Kuomintang armies approached, the workers went on strike, sabotaged factories, damaged foreign business houses and then rose in revolt against the forces of the war-lords. As a result, Chiang's armies had much quicker success than they had hoped for. By the end of March 1927 they were in Shanghai, with all of China south of the Yangtse in their hands.

The Shanghai Massacres

Chiang now decided to turn on the Communists. He had several reasons. The transfer of land was turning the gentry against the Kuomintang. The strength of the trade unions meant that he was losing the goodwill of the businessmen who financed his armies. But, above all, he knew that the Communists were using him to defeat the war-lords and would then rise against the Kuomintang. The Russian leader, Stalin, made this perfectly plain in a speech in Moscow. 'The Right', he said, 'have to be utilized to the end, squeezed dry like a lemon and then flung away.'

Chiang had no intention of being flung away. He called on his friends amongst the Shanghai gangs for help, and, just one week after Stalin's speech, they and some of his troops began a massacre of Communists. Communist offices were raided and Party officials arrested and shot, trade union leaders and strike pickets were killed in the streets; anyone sympathetic to the Communists suffered the same fate. Similar massacres took place in all Kuomintang-held cities. Thousands lost their lives in this horrible episode, and the few remaining Communists had to go into hiding.

The Left Kuomintang made a few weak efforts to stop the massacres. They tried to expel Chiang from the Kuomintang

Joseph Stalin, leader of Soviet Russia after Lenin's death.
Above him is a portrait of Karl Marx

but he, not they, commanded the armies. Soon they were meekly accepting his orders and agreeing that Borodin and his staff should be sent back to Russia.

Chiang was now the complete master of the Kuomintang, a party in which the Right was by far the strongest group.

The War-lords Defeated

In late 1927 Chiang's armies marched towards Peking on the second stage of the Northern Expedition. This, too, was a swift campaign and there was almost no opposition. The most serious trouble came, not from the war-lords, but from the Japanese. The route passed through Shantung, the district seized by Japan under the Twenty-one Demands.

Chiang ordered that care should be taken to avoid quarrels, but fighting broke out between Japanese and Chinese troops in Tsinan. In the street battle that followed a thousand troops

74

and civilians were killed. Chiang withdrew his men quickly
and the army passed on without further trouble, but the bad
feeling that had been created was a sign of evil times to come.

In 1928 the Kuomintang entered Peking and the Northern
Expedition was over. Chiang decided that the proper capital
for the new government of China was Nanking, the town
where Sun Yat-sen had set up the first Republic. Sun's body
was taken to a huge tomb overlooking the town.

Chiang was still faced with the problem of the war-lords
who had fled before the advancing Kuomintang armies into
Manchuria and the north-west. The Japanese obligingly
assassinated the 'Old Marshal', who held Manchuria, in the
hope that his son, the 'Young Marshal', would break away
from China and rule Manchuria under their influence. But
the Young Marshal declared his loyalty to the Nanking
government. In the north-west, the ruling war-lord was
General Feng, often known as the 'Christian General' and

General Feng Yu-hsiang, the 'Christian General' with Chiang
Kai-shek

famous for using a hose-pipe to baptize heathen troops.[1] Feng did not want to give up his private army and rose against Chiang with a force of 600,000 men. Chiang sent his best troops against him and, after six months fighting and the death of 150,000 of his men, Feng surrendered.

This was the end of serious opposition from the war-lords. Chiang, it seemed, was firmly in the saddle. 'After this', he wrote, 'there never can rise in the future any militarists who dare destroy unity and revolt against the Kuomintang and the government.'

But it was too early to be so optimistic. Chiang had two enemies who turned out to be very much stronger than anyone could have imagined. They were the Communists and the Japanese. The next two chapters explain how they threatened the security of the Kuomintang government.

[1] The story that Feng baptized his troops with a hose-pipe is based on a joke he once made and is probably not true.

10 The Communists Begin Again

The Autumn Harvest Uprising

After the Shanghai Massacre, the surviving Communists knew that, unless they acted quickly, their support in the villages and towns would wither away altogether. They decided on a desperate effort to build up a peasant army and seize a few cities in Hunan. Mao Tse-tung's task was to capture Changsha, the town he knew so well.

The first stage of this 'Autumn Harvest Uprising' was successful. Mao raised four 'Workers and Peasants Revolutionary Armies' and marched on Changsha. But the trade unions in the town failed to rise in support, and two of his armies were crushed by the Kuomintang forces. Mao himself was captured but, by a lucky chance, his captors did not recognize him and allowed him to buy his freedom. He then walked for several days until he came up with about a thousand men, the sole remnants of his four armies. These he led into a remote mountain district known as Chinghanshan. In the next few months he was joined there by the other Communist leaders and the battered remnants of their armies. By the spring of 1928 there were more than 10,000 troops in Chinghanshan.

They controlled a plateau about twenty-five miles wide, covered with thick pine forests and linked with the outside world only by five narrow and steep mountain paths. There were five villages on the plateau, inhabited by people so primitive that they had no knowledge of metals. In the woods tigers, leopards and wolves roamed. It was a wild place but a safe stronghold, and here Mao set up the first Chinese Communist state.

It was called the Kiangsi-Hunan Soviet; 'soviet' being the Russian term for a republic ruled by a council of workers,

77

peasants and soldiers. For six years this little independent state survived under Mao's leadership. He sent reports of their progress to Communist Party leaders who had moved into underground headquarters in Shanghai.

The Kiangsi-Hunan Soviet

Mao reported that living conditions were hard:

'In addition to grain each man receives only five cents a day for cooking oil, salt, firewood and vegetables, and even this is hard to keep up. We now have cotton padding for winter clothing for the whole army of five thousand men but are short of cloth. Cold as the weather is, many of our men are still wearing only two layers of thin clothing. . . . all of us share the same hardships; from the commander of the army to the cook everyone lives on the daily food allowance. . . . Also many officers and men have fallen ill from malnutrition, exposure to cold and other causes. Our hospitals up in the mountains give both Chinese and Western treatment but are short of doctors and medicines.'

Nevertheless their spirit was good because it was a democratic community: 'The officers do not beat the men; officers and soldiers receive equal treatment; soldiers are free to hold meetings and speak out; trivial formalities have been done away with; and the accounts are open for all to inspect.'

They were not content to stay in their mountain stronghold, but began to infiltrate into the surrounding villages to persuade the peasants to take over the government of the villages themselves. They encouraged them to band together to confiscate the land of the landlords:

'Roughly speaking, more than 60 per cent of the land belonged to the landlords and less than 40 per cent to the peasants. . . . The township is taken as the unit for land distribution. . . . All the inhabitants, men and women, old and young, received equal shares.'

They found it was a mistake to treat the richer peasants and small town merchants in the same way as the very rich landlords, as they went over to Chiang's 'White' Forces:

'The ultra-Left policy of attacking the petty bourgeoisie drove most of them to the side of the landlords, with the result that they put on white ribbons and opposed us. With the gradual change of this policy the situation has been steadily improving. . . . The merchants in the county town and other market towns no longer fight shy of us and quite a few speak well of the Red Army. The landlords imposed very heavy taxes and tolls on the people; the pacification guards [anti-communist forces set up by the landlords] of Suichan levied five toll charges along the seventy-li [twenty-three mile] road from Hungao to Tsaolin, no farm produce being exempt. We crushed the pacification guards and abolished these tolls, thus winning the support of all the peasants as well as of small and middle merchants.'

The most important part of Mao's report described the tactics they used to deal with the constantly threatening White armies. The Red Army, Mao said, was the first in history to take on a double task. It had to defend itself against the enemy, but it was also a propaganda force sent into the countryside to win over the people to communism. 'These tactics are like casting a net; at any moment we should be able to cast it out or draw it in. We cast it wide to win over the masses and draw it in to deal with the enemy.'

When an enemy attack was launched the Communists avoided meeting it in pitched battle. Instead, they used guerrilla tactics, breaking into small mobile groups which concealed themselves in the hills and attacked when the enemy was unprepared or weary after a long march. Mao simplified these tactics into four easily remembered lines:

> The enemy attacks, we retreat;
> The enemy camps, we harass;
> The enemy tires; we attack;
> The enemy retreats; we pursue.

The Encirclement Campaigns

The Communists were once again a threat to Chiang Kai-shek. He was determined to crush them before they built up their strength again. After he had put down the last of the war-lords in 1930, he launched his armies in the first of five attempts to encircle and wipe out the Kiangsi-Hunan Soviet. Mao's guerrilla tactics were to be put to a severe test.

As Chiang's men advanced through the countryside

surrounding the Red stronghold, they found the peasants were sympathetic towards the Communists. They were showing their gratitude to the Red Army for the help it had given in redistributing land and driving out the greediest landlords. Thousands of peasants left their villages and joined the Red Army in the hills. Others stayed on to give false directions and lead Chiang's forces into ambushes. Guerrilla bands attacked small White detachments without warning, and slipped away into the night with captured weapons before the soldiers had time to rally.

Despite these difficulties, Chiang's army pressed on into the mountainous area. When they had advanced a long way from their base and were well strung out, the guerrilla bands were secretly called together to make up one large force. In two surprise attacks they smashed the Kuomintang armies. The booty collected by the Communists from this first Encircle-ment Campaign amounted to 6,000 rifles, several million rounds of ammunition, and three thousand prisoners who were willing to desert to the Reds. They also captured two radio sets which, at first, they could not use, as no Red soldier had ever seen one before.

Within months Chiang launched a second Encirclement Campaign. This time the Communists' booty amounted to 20,000 prisoners and an equal number of rifles. The third campaign began a month later, in September 1931, and had developed into the familiar game of hide and seek when Chiang called it off. He had to turn his attention to his other enemy — Japan.

11 Manchuria

In the early evening of 18 September 1931 a Japanese major-general left the railway station in Mukden, the capital of Manchuria. There was still time to take the despatches he was carrying to the local commander of the Japanese troops but he, nevertheless, made straight for a tea-house. Several hours later he was still there, obviously reluctant to leave and continue his journey. Suddenly, the night quiet was shattered by the blast of an explosion, followed by rapid rifle fire. Of all the customers, only the major-general remained calm. To most people in Mukden that night the explosion was a cause for alarm. To the major-general and a few others it was a sign that what was later to be known as the 'Mukden incident' had been successfully staged. The next morning the major-general could present the orders he was carrying from the war office in Tokyo. They absolutely forbade the Japanese army to go ahead with its plan for the conquest of Manchuria. It was already too late; the action of a few irresponsible men had dragged Japan into a course of violence which ended only when the atom bombs fell on Japanese cities in 1945.

Japan Seizes Manchuria

Manchuria had been a Chinese province for three hundred years. It was a fertile grain-producing region and China's most important source of coal and iron. For a quarter of a century it had been Japan's ambition to put this wealth to her own use.

In 1905 she had been granted the lease of Port Arthur and the right to build the South Manchuria Railway. In 1915, as part of the Twenty-one Demands, she had been given the right to own mines and iron and steel works in Manchuria. During the war-lord period she had further strengthened her position. The Old Marshal had raised no objection as more Japanese businesses were opened and troops were moved into

81

the area to 'protect' Japanese interests.

Then the Japanese had quarrelled with the Old Marshal and, foolishly, arranged for his assassination. They believed that the Young Marshal, who was then a weak character addicted to opium, would be an even more obedient puppet than his father. The Young Marshal, however, was shaken by these events into pulling himself together. He cured himself of his opium addiction, and began to defend the interests of the Chinese in Manchuria against the Japanese infiltration. When he declared his loyalty to Chiang Kai-shek in 1930, the Japanese knew they had no hope of gradually winning control over the entire industry and agriculture of Manchuria.

The officers of the Japanese army in China, without their government's knowledge, prepared a plan for the military occupation of all Manchuria. Their excuse was to be a faked attack on Japanese troops. By the autumn of 1931 all was ready, when the government in Tokyo heard rumours of the plan. The Prime Minister ordered the cancellation of the plot, but the messenger chosen to carry his orders was in league with his brother officers. Travelling with deliberate slowness, he still arrived in Mukden a few hours too soon; but the visit to the tea-house conveniently explained why the letters were not delivered to the commander-in-chief until after the incident.

Then it was too late. The army had blown up a section of the Japanese-owned South Manchuria Railway, and claimed that this was the work of Chinese saboteurs. They had, they said, fired on the escaping saboteurs but had failed to capture any of them. By the next morning, Japanese troops were already advancing towards Mukden to take revenge for the supposed attack. It was, in fact, the beginning of a well planned conquest of the whole of Manchuria. Within five months the Young Marshal and his armies had been driven south of the Great Wall.

For the sake of appearances, Japan declared Manchuria an independent kingdom with the new name of Manchukuo. They even found it a king—the Manchu Emperor who had been forced to abdicate by Sun Yat-sen and Yuan Shi-kai in 1912. But he ruled under direct orders from the commander of the Japanese forces in Manchuria, and everyone knew that

Japan had stolen China's richest province by force of arms. The only source of comfort to Chinese pride was that they had, after brave fighting, beaten off an attack made by the Japanese navy on Shanghai and thus saved the south of China from invasion.

Chiang and Japan

Two days after the Mukden incident, Chiang appealed to the League of Nations. The League had been set up in 1919 to preserve world peace and could call on member states to provide an international force to deal with aggressors. A League

Posters such as these were displayed throughout Japan to persuade Japanese people to emigrate to Manchukuo. They suggest that Manchukuo was a fertile land where poor farmers would prosper and provide plentiful food and luxuries for their families

Commission of Enquiry reported that Japan had no justifica-
tion for its attack and she was ordered to evacuate Manchuria.
None of the League's members, however, was prepared to use
force, or even to stop trading with Japan until she obeyed.
Japan simply resigned from the League and stayed in Manchuria.

So Chiang had to deal with her on his own. He had plenty
of support in China for any action he decided to take. The
Manchurian affair led to yet another storm of bitter anti-
Japanese feeling and the cry went up, particularly from
students, for Chiang to lead an all-out attack to resist the
invaders.

He disappointed them by taking no action against the
Japanese. Chiang believed that China was still too weak to
tackle such a powerful enemy without help from other nations.
He feared that an attack on the Japanese in Manchuria would
lead to all-out war between the two countries and an invasion
of the rest of China which his armies could not possibly resist.
At all costs, he thought, China must avoid antagonizing
Japan for the next few years. She might, in this way, gain
sufficient time to build her strength and be prepared for a
successful reconquest of Manchuria.

This view brought many angry protests, particularly when
it appeared that Chiang, while he was not prepared to fight
the Japanese, did intend to continue the campaigns against the
Communists. His opponents argued that the Communists were
no serious menace, locked up in their tiny mountain stronghold, while the Japanese could use Manchuria as a base for
further aggression against China.

But Chiang insisted that his way was right. In 1932 he sent
his armies to make their fourth attempt to overrun the
Kiangsi-Hunan Soviet.

Postscript—Manchuria and World War II

The Manchurian affair showed the Japanese army and naval
officers that it was possible to defy their government. They
were encouraged by their success to demand that Japan
should take up a warlike policy towards all her Far Eastern
neighbours. Any resistance to this disastrous idea was met
with violence. In 1932 the Prime Minister was assassinated by

Japanese troops on the march in China. The year after their capture of Manchuria they added the neighbouring area of Jehol to their Chinese possessions

a gang of young officers, and he was merely one of many Japanese leaders who met a similar fate.

Gradually, the militarists gained control of the government and set up a police state in which free speech became impossible. Through their control of the press, the cinema and education, they turned Japan into a nation bent on conquest. It was this nation which attacked China again in 1937 and, four years later, made the treacherous attack on American ships at Pearl Harbour. The Japanese call the years from 1931 to 1945 the 'Dark Valley', because they were a shameful period, between the honest attempts at democratic government of the 1920s and the new freedom and democracy which have grown up since 1945.

The failure of the League of Nations to stop aggression in Manchuria had grave consequences in Europe, too. Both Germany and Italy noted that Japan's aggression had been met only with words. The lesson was plain; there was no power in the world prepared to stop a determined aggressor.

In 1934 Germany followed Japan's lead and resigned from the League of Nations. In 1936 she invaded the Rhineland in the first of a series of attacks on her European neighbours. Meanwhile, Italy was conquering Abyssinia, a powerless African country to which she had no more right than the Japanese had to Manchuria. Thus, three nations were launched on a path of conquest which led directly to the Second World War.

12 The Long March

The first three Encirclement Campaigns taught Chiang to be wary of the guerrillas. In the fourth campaign he kept his half million troops together so that they could not be attacked in small units. Instead of allowing his men to be drawn into the mountains, he concentrated on forcing the Communists to evacuate the surrounding plains. This tactic was a success. The Reds were forced to retreat and, in preparation for the fifth campaign, Chiang set up a tight blockade of the mountain stronghold. The populations of whole villages were moved behind his troops, so that they could no longer supply the Communists with food or pass on information about troop movements. To prevent sudden Communist raids a ring of blockhouses, or small forts, one or two miles apart, was built.

The besieged Communists soon began to feel the effects of the blockade. Rations fell to fourteen ounces a day; certain important items like salt became nearly unobtainable. Clearly they could not hold out much longer and, on 2 October 1934, they took the momentous decision to evacuate before they were crushed by the forthcoming fifth campaign.

Equipment was hastily packed; not only guns and radio sets, but sewing machines, lathes and printing presses were to be taken. No one had many personal belongings. All Mao owned in the world was a sun helmet, a torn umbrella, two uniforms, one cotton sheet, two blankets, a water jug and a rice bowl. But as he was Chairman Mao, the head of the government, he also carried a knapsack divided into nine compartments. Each held papers or maps connected with the affairs of his state. For four years he had had no better office than a cave, and very often only a flat stone on a hillside. But even the primitive conditions in the Kiangsi-Hunan Soviet were luxurious compared with the cruel ordeal that lay ahead.

In the next twelve months Mao and his comrades were to undertake one of the toughest adventures known to history.

The Long March

At first the Communists intended to march only a few hundred miles to set up a new base to the north-west of their old position. But the fierce attacks that Chiang made on the marching column proved that he now held the advantage in southern China. A halt was made, while Mao and the Red Army generals reconsidered their plans. It seemed that they could only find safety in the mountainous country north of the Yangtse, so they took the incredible decision to march to the province of Shensi, 6,000 miles away. To give their men heart for the fearsome journey, they explained that the Red Army would then be able to play its part in resisting the hated Japanese in Manchuria. 'Go north to fight the Japanese' was

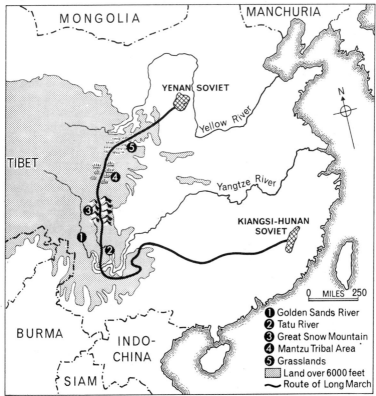

The Long March. The route taken by Mao and the main body of Communist forces, 1934-1935

87

the slogan which drove every soldier on in the cruel months that followed.

The Rivers

Both Mao and Chiang knew that, unless it could cross the Yangtse, it was only a matter of time before the Red Army was annihilated. A desperate race took place; the Communists making forced marches of up to forty miles a day, under constant attack from Chiang's troops and his air force of a hundred or so planes. In the first three weeks twenty-five thousand men were killed, and the army had to be split into several columns to spread out the target they presented to the Whites.

As they neared the Yangtse, it was reported that Chiang had assembled enough troops in their path to make it impossible for them to press forward. So they turned and marched to the west, until they were south of the point where the Golden Sands River and the Tatu River join to form the Yangtse.

Here they suddenly turned and struck north again, straight for the Golden Sands River. Chiang sent the White army in pursuit. He ordered the boats at every crossing place to be taken to the north bank, where a huge body of Kuomintang troops gathered. Others were despatched to attack the Communists from the rear.

It appeared that they were trapped again; but what the Reds lacked in equipment and numbers they made up in speed and cunning. The main force halted at the river and began to build a bridge, as though preparing for a crossing. Meanwhile, one battalion undertook a forced march, reaching a village eighty-five miles to the west after only a day and night. Here, on the north bank, a few Kuomintang soldiers were guarding half a dozen boats. A few of the Communists appeared on the south bank, dressed in Kuomintang officers' uniforms, and called for a boat to be sent over. In this they crossed the river, attacked the sleepy soldiers guarding the five remaining boats, and sent them over to their waiting comrades.

During the next nine days the boats ceaselessly crossed and recrossed the river, transporting one battalion after another as each reached the new crossing place. They then burned the boats and marched towards the Tatu. If the Whites knew what was happening they showed little energy in preventing it. It was another two days before they arrived on the scene.

The Tatu flows deep and fast through steep, narrow gorges, and boat crossings are almost impossible. The Communists tried with three boats. Two of them sank and the third took four hours to battle against the wild, erratic currents. So they marched upstream to the Luting bridge. This had been constructed by simply throwing chains from one bank to the other and laying planks across them. When the Reds arrived the planks had gone, and at the other end of the swaying chains a Kuomintang machine gun post had been set up. Nevertheless, volunteers eagerly stepped forward. A Communist general later recalled their bravery:

'I remember the bridge was about 140 metres wide with six or seven iron chains placed about thirty centimetres apart. It was a shaky bridge at all times and the current was too strong for us to cross by rafts or pontoons. So the soldiers crossed one by one, hanging down from the bridge, hand over hand, their only weapons hand grenades and pistols, for a rifle would be useless. The current was terribly fast. The bridge was a hundred metres above the level of the water. I cannot remember very much but I remember the people falling into the water, and there was nothing we could do to help them.'

A handful of soldiers did survive this nightmare and succeeded in reaching the far end of the bridge to overpower the machine gunners. The planks were replaced and the entire Red Army walked across.

They were now reasonably safe from Chiang's armies, but the journey was only half completed. On the second stage the enemy was not the Kuomintang but some of Asia's most inhospitable country.

The Mountains and Grasslands

First, they struggled over the 16,000 feet Great Snow Mountain:

'Men died on top of the mountain. They would be standing next to you and talking to you, and then their face took on a sudden frozen look, they swayed and they were dead; and what was extraordinary was that some of the strongest men died on the mountain.'

Those who survived this ordeal passed on through the r.erve-stretching eeriness of the border lands between Tibet and China. Unseen primitive tribesmen fired poisoned arrows at any one rash enough to stray from the main party. Rocks were rolled down on them from the tops of cliffs. They met no one with whom they could trade for food; and they were reduced to eating unripe wheat, stolen from the small patches of cultivated fields.

All agreed that the Grasslands were the worst. These were a foul black bog covered with a thick carpet of coarse grass:

'Treacherous bogs were everywhere, which sucked a man down once he stepped off the firmer parts and more quickly if he tried to extricate himself. We could only advance with minute care stepping on grass clumps. Even so, one could not help feeling very nervous for the great grass mounds sank with the pressure and black water would rise and submerge the foot.'

It was too dangerous to lie down. They slept standing back to back to hold each other erect. The torrential rain was continuous; and, of course, there was no food: 'We killed our oxen and horses for meat, and carried them on our few remaining baggage animals, and then in the end we ate the baggage animals and carried the meat ourselves.'

It was the worst of the horrors of the March, but it was the last. A few weeks later they reached their destination; just below the Great Wall in the north of Shensi province.

After some months they decided to make the city of Yenan the headquarters of a new Communist state—the Shensi Soviet. It remained the centre of Communist activities in China until they became masters of the whole country in 1949.

What Did They Achieve?

The Long March is one of the greatest feats of endurance in history. The Red Army covered six thousand miles in three hundred and eighty-six days. They had rested for about a hundred of these, which meant that an average day's march had equalled twenty-four miles. On many days they must have done more, for they had stopped frequently to fight.

There had been fifteen days of major battle and hardly one without a skirmish or two. The Communists crossed eighteen mountain ranges, twenty-four rivers and several swamps and deserts. They passed through eleven provinces and occupied sixty cities.

One hundred thousand men set off with Mao. Only twenty thousand survived to march with him into Shensi. What had they achieved?

First, the survival of Chinese communism. After being so nearly crushed in the south, the Party had re-established itself in a new base from which it was never dislodged. Secondly, they had carried their faith to the people of some of the remotest regions of China. While the soldiers had fought, political instructors had explained communism, encouraged the people to seize landlords' farms and shown them how to take the government of their villages into their own hands. They had left behind units of armed peasants who had been given a quick course in guerrilla fighting. They would be useful to the Communists in future struggles with Chiang. Mao summed up their success:

'The Long March is also an agitation corps. It declares to the approximately two hundred million people of eleven provinces that only the road of the Red Army leads to their liberation. Without the Long March, how could the people of the broad masses have known so quickly that there are such great ideas in the world as are upheld by the Red Army?'

For Mao the March had been a mixture of triumph and tragedy. He had been severely ill with fever during the crossing of the Great Snow Mountain. His wife, one of the thirty women on the March, had been carried on a stretcher for ten months after she had been injured in a bombing raid. Worse, they had been forced to hand over three of their children to the care of peasants. They were never seen again.

It had been a triumph for his political ideas. Before the March he had been out of favour with the leaders of the Party, who had gone underground in Shanghai. They had disapproved of the Kiangsi-Hunan Soviet which was built on the support of peasants. Karl Marx had taught that peasants could never make a true revolutionary force, which could only arise among the working class of industrial cities—the *proletariat*. Some of Mao's critics argued that the idea of a peasant revolution was not communism at all. The Russians, for instance, had no faith in 'Maoism' and gave no help to the Reds on the Long March.

Indeed they sent no more help to any Chinese Communists for, after the success of the Long March, the Party was united under Mao's leadership. Some of the old leaders left the Party, others came to work for Mao at Yenan. From 1935 onwards there was never any serious challenge to his position as the head of the Chinese Communist Party.

13 China in the 1930s

The Record of the Kuomintang

How well had Chiang Kai-shek and the Kuomintang ruled China since they came to power in 1928? They had promised to carry out the programme of reform laid down by Sun Yat-sen and had encouraged the idolization of his memory. His body had been reburied, with great ceremony, in a magnificent tomb on a mountain overlooking the new capital, Nanking. Each week his will was read out in schools and every child had to study the *Three Principles of the People*. His portrait hung in every classroom and office.

Chiang had hoped that the Chinese would look on him as the natural successor to Sun. He had, after all, been closest to Sun when he was in great danger, and had followed him as leader of the Kuomintang. In 1927 he had married Mayling Soong, Madame Sun's sister. But what really counted, of course, was how far he had carried on Sun's battle against

The body of Sun Yat-sen is carried to its new resting place

the backwardness of China and the cruelty and oppression suffered by her people.

Observers who visited only the coastal cities felt that the Kuomintang had lifted China straight into the modern world. They noticed the gay life, the European clothes worn by young men and women, the spread of such amusements as the cinema and radio. Women of the better-off families were freer; their feet were no longer bound and brides arranged their own marriages. Girls were educated, and schooling for both girls and boys had broken away from the dead and useless learning of Sun's day.

There were new factories; many owned by Chinese and not by foreigners. Everyone agreed that there had been a tremendous improvement in communications. The railway system had been extended and more than fifty thousand miles of motor roads built. Most of these ran through the coastal areas; travel into the interior was eased by the development of airways.

These changes impressed Western visitors and won China many friends. The feeling grew, particularly in the United States, that China was no longer the sick nation of the East, but a country whose struggles deserved respect and help. This sympathy increased in many quarters when Chiang

An obvious result of Kuomintang government. Chinese students in Paris wearing the typical western dress of the 1930s

announced his conversion to Christianity in 1930 and was seen to welcome missionaries, and schools and colleges set up by Christians.

Support from the West made it possible for Chiang to carry out one of Sun's aims; the cancellation of the leases to foreigners. By a series of agreements the powers ended their leases, gave up extra-territorial rights and returned the customs service to Chinese control.

The struggle for the People's Nationalism was won; but very little progress was made towards establishing the other two principles.

The People's Livelihood

The greatest social problem had always been the poverty and oppression suffered by the Chinese peasant. Chiang did nothing to lessen these evils. Sun had stated that the People's Livelihood depended on carrying out the 'land to the tiller' policy. This Chiang dare not do, because he depended too much on the support of the landlords. After the Communist evacuation of the Kiangsi-Hunan Soviet, he helped the land-lords to take back their lands by force. Nothing was done to stop the old cruel practices. Landlords still charged excessive rents and tax collectors overcharged the peasants. The man-darins disappeared, but their place was taken by village head-men, who were always landlords and just as oppressive to the people.

For the peasant and for the poor townsman there was no real improvement under the Kuomintang. It failed to pro-vide schools for the poor; nothing was done to care for the sick and the aged. Sun had dreamed of bringing tractors and electricity to the service of the peasants. The Kuomintang took no steps to spread such benefits to the countryside.

Even in a town like Shanghai, where at first glance every-thing seemed bright, gay and modern, the improvements brought by the Kuomintang were a sham. They benefited only the wealthy, whose new homes, shopping centres and cinemas took visitors' minds off some of the world's foulest slums. The bodies of twenty thousand of Shanghai's poor were gathered each year from the streets where they had died of starvation, overwork and disease.

95

There were three Soong sisters. On the right stands Chingling Soong, Madame Sun. Mayling Soong, Chiang's wife is in the centre. The third sister is Eiling Soong, the wife of Dr Kung, an important figure in the Kuomintang

The People's Democracy

Sun had seen that in the early years the Kuomintang would have to be in sole control of the government. But he had laid down that it was the Kuomintang's duty to lead the Chinese towards democracy and, in the end, to allow them to vote for their own rulers.

This never happened under Chiang. The Kuomintang remained in sole control of all government posts. There was no parliament and even the Kuomintang officials could not speak their mind. They took their orders from Chiang Kaishek, the Party leader, and a few of his close associates.

Chiang was kept in power by the activities of his secret police, the Blue Shirts. The press was censored so that all criticism was stifled. China was becoming unhappily similar to Mussolini's Italy and Hitler's Germany. Chiang admired both these men. He had a copy of Mussolini's biography given to each army officer.

His supporters claimed that his dictatorship was justified by the need to hold the country together in the face of the Japanese and Communist threat. But his critics pointed out that this didn't excuse the dishonesty and corruption that he allowed to spread. It was frequently said that China's affairs were in the hands of four wealthy families, one headed by Chiang himself and two of the others by his wife's brother and brother-in-law. These millionaires were accused of using their government positions to line their own pockets, thus setting a pattern for other businessmen to follow. It was impossible to be successful in business unless you were in the Kuomintang. Black marketeering went on at all levels, particularly during the shortages of wartime.

The People's Livelihood and the People's Democracy were as far away in 1945 as they were in 1928. Chiang had not proved himself a worthy successor to Sun. Madame Sun always considered that Chiang had betrayed the trust her husband had placed in him, and refused to have any connection with the Kuomintang. Sun Fo also realized that his father would not have approved. In 1944 he said:

'We must frankly admit the fact that in these twenty years the machinery and practice of the Kuomintang have turned in a wrong direction, inconsistent with the Party Constitution drafted by Dr Sun Yat-sen in 1923 and contrary to the spirit of democracy.'

The Red Border Region

Many Westerners visited China in the 1930s but very few travelled as far as the Yenan Border Region where Mao had set up a communist soviet. The journey was difficult, but Chiang had other reasons for discouraging visits there. According to the reports circulated by the Kuomintang, the Reds were a small struggling group of bandits, terrorizing the north-west of China, cruel, ignorant and incapable of proper government. The handful of journalists who actually visited the Region found that the truth was far different. The area was indeed poor, but it lacked the terror and misery which were common throughout the rest of the Chinese countryside. The Region was well governed, taxes were low and the peasants contented.

They were impressed by the activity in the Border Region. When the Communists had arrived there had been no industry at all; but the sewing machines, lathes and presses carried on the Long March were soon busy in the first small work-

97

shops. After eight years there was industrial work for 200,000 men and women.

The Region still depended chiefly on its farmers, who were happier here than anywhere else in China. This was because their rents were fixed at a reasonable level by the Communists and it was possible for the tenant of even a small farm to make a living. Places had been found for the landless on the new farms carved out of uncultivated land with the help of communist agricultural experts. Peasants now found it worth while to improve their methods and the food and cotton production of the Region had risen enormously.

Although he had cut the landlords' profits, Mao would not allow their land to be taken from them by force as he had done in the Kiangsi-Hunan Soviet. As the Communists were demanding a united front with the Kuomintang against Japan, it was important to appear as moderate reformers, not as revolutionaries bent on seizing all the property of the rich. Yet, of course, to Mao the reforms in the Yenan Border Region were only one step towards the goal of a communist revolution. Privately, he knew that one day the Communists would violently overthrow the landlords. Revolutions, to a Marxist, are only made by violence, and Mao himself had once said: '. . . a revolution is not the same as inviting people to dinner, or writing an essay or painting a picture or doing fancy needlework; it cannot be anything so refined, so calm and

A doctor stands in front of his cave surgery in Yenan

gentle. . . . A revolution is an act of violence whereby one class overthrows another.'

Mao governed the Border Region from his dwelling in the hills overlooking Yenan. Yenan was a large city, but Kuomintang and Japanese bombing raids drove the Communists to the shelters that were easily scraped out of the soft yellow rock. In such a cave Mao worked, slept and ate his peasant meals of millet, rice and vegetables. Dressed in shabby cotton clothes, he grew vegetables and tobacco in a small garden and insisted that all Communist leaders should do some similar manual labour. He set an example by working for thirteen or fourteen hours a day, ceaselessly planning the next steps in the revolution.

He taught his followers that they had four main tasks to carry out:

The Cadres

A very large number of Party cadres had to be trained. A cadre was a Communist who thoroughly understood his Party's tactics and could be relied on to carry them out. He had to be capable of working among non-communists and it was through his work that the party would gain support among the masses.

The training went on daily. Workers, peasants and soldiers, men and women, finished work and then attended meetings of their party cell or lectures by Party leaders. An intensive propaganda campaign was kept up, using posters, newspapers and even plays and operas to explain the party line.

The Peasants

The peasants were the raw material out of which the revolution would be made. The Party had to win their support by showing that it understood their problems. The cadres should gain their confidence and prepare them for the day when they should rise against the landlords.

The Red Army

The Red Army must become the strongest and the best trained in China. There could be no communist success without a strong army. 'Political power', Mao emphasized,

Students learning resistance songs outside their university in the caves at Yenan

'grows out of the barrel of a gun.'

The Japanese War

The Communists must play the major part in resisting the Japanese. By showing themselves as the defenders of the Chinese people they would win widespread support. Mao welcomed the fact that the war was likely to be a long drawn-out struggle. The longer it lasted, the more the Kuomintang armies would be weakened. The Communists, on the other hand, by using their guerrilla tactics could keep their armies intact. They would then be ready to overthrow the Kuomintang once Japan was defeated.

14 Sian

The Red Bandits

Chiang had no intention of letting the Communists alone now that they were established in Yenan. There were many signs that the Japanese were preparing to take over a large area of north China, but he ignored this danger and ordered a campaign to suppress the Red Bandits, as they were called by the Kuomintang press.

For 'Commander of Bandit Suppression' Chiang made a foolish choice. He appointed Chang Hsueh-liang,[1] the Young Marshal. Chang's heart was not in the task. He wanted revenge for his defeat in Manchuria and for the assassination of his father. The Japanese, and not his own countrymen, were his enemy. The Communists played on his feelings. After

[1] Pronounced Jong Schweh-liahng.

Chang Hsueh-liang, the 'Young Marshal'

they had won a couple of battles, Mao ordered fighting to stop. He returned prisoners captured from Chang's army. They had been drilled with communist slogans: 'Form an anti-Japanese front', 'Fight back to Manchuria'. They reported to Chang that the Communists were sincere in wanting to fight the Japanese.

In October 1936 Chang refused to go on any longer with bandit suppression. Chiang was furious at this and left Nanking to fly out himself to Chang's headquarters in Sian.

Mutiny

He landed on 4 December, accompanied by several officials and a bodyguard of forty-five men. He immediately went into conference with Chang, and made it clear that he was still not prepared to fight the Japanese until the Communists had been destroyed.

Early in the morning of 12 December, men from the Young Marshal's army moved silently through the streets of Sian and arrested all known supporters of Chiang. They then burst into the hotel where he and his bodyguard were staying. The sound of firing awoke Chiang. He left by a back door and clambered up the snow-covered hillside behind the hotel. An hour or so later his pursuers found him huddled, shivering, in a hollow, wearing only a night-shirt. They took him back to Chang's headquarters, where he waited to be taken out and shot.

But the Young Marshal knew that Chiang was the only leader capable of reconciling the old war-lords to a war against the Japanese. If he died they would begin quarrelling amongst themselves again. He did not intend to kill Chiang, but to make him change his mind. A plane was sent to Yenan to ask for a leading Communist to come and negotiate with his prisoner.

The man they sent was Chou En-lai.[1] He had good reason to hate Chiang, for he had nearly lost his life in the Shanghai massacres. He had been spared at the last minute by the officer in charge of a firing squad, who recognized him as an old friend. Now he concealed his bitterness. His job was not to gloat over the unfortunate prisoner, but to persuade him to

[1] Pronounced Joe En-lie.

The snow-covered hill where Chiang was captured

agree to the Communist proposal for a united front of Communists and Kuomintang.

Chiang was in no position to turn down the offer. He was not allowed to leave Sian until he had agreed to call off the anti-communist campaign and accept Red Army help against the Japanese. Only then was he allowed to fly back to Nanking with his wife, who had bravely flown out to join him in captivity. Before leaving Nanking she had probably saved Chiang's life by persuading the Kuomintang leaders not to bomb Sian. This had been their first thought on hearing of the plot, and shows that they assumed the Chiang would have been immediately killed by the Young Marshal.

The Young Marshal also returned with Chiang. Having mutinied against his commander-in-chief, he had volunteered to fly back with him as his prisoner. By doing so he saved Chiang from losing face. He was repaid for his gesture by being kept a close prisoner for the next twenty-five years.

The United Front

The details of the agreement between Chiang and the Communists were worked out in the spring of 1937. The main points were:

1. Chiang called off the suppression campaign and agreed that the Communists should remain in control of their Soviet, which was to be known as the 'Border Region'.
2. In return, the Communists agreed not to oppose the Kuomintang government. They also promised to stop the confiscation of land from landowners.
3. The Red Army was to remain in existence, but it would fight the Japanese under the orders of the national government.
4. A Council made up of representatives of the Kuomintang and the Communists, with some independent members of no party, was set up to organize the war against Japan.

Neither side kept fully to the agreement, but there was no mistaking its meaning; the Chinese nation was united for war. Japan gave China no further time to prepare her forces. In July 1937 she attacked Chinese troops stationed at the Marco Polo bridge, just outside Peking, thus beginning the all-out war which lasted until 1945.

15 The War against Japan

The Japanese Onslaught 1937–8

In one rapid campaign, Japanese columns swept from their landing point at Tientsin into the provinces of northern China. There was little resistance, and they were soon masters of the whole of the northern plain, the most thickly populated region of the country.

Their next objective was the Yangtse river. Control of its valley would give them the great cities and a highway pointing straight into the heart of China. Chiang tried to prevent this by striking at the Japanese forces in Shanghai, the natural starting place for a Yangtse campaign. For two months a ghastly struggle went on, winning for the Chinese soldier the

Foreign business continued while Chinese and Japanese troops fought for control of Shanghai

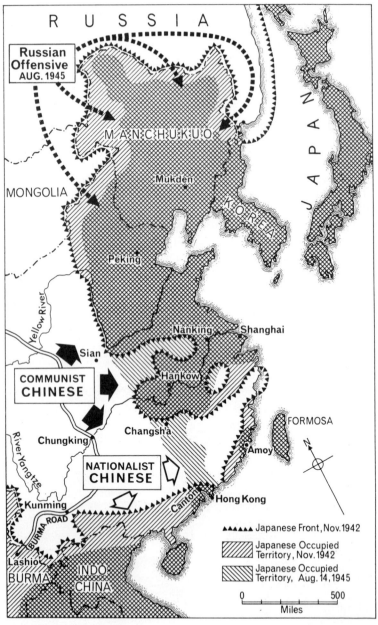

The War against Japan

admiration of the world. It was a battle of flesh against steel and high explosive; the Chinese soldier, armed only with a rifle, standing up heroically to the machine guns, the heavy artillery and the air bombardment of the Japanese. Although tens of thousands died, Chiang's men held out, forcing the Japanese to out-manoeuvre them by landing further south and sweeping round Shanghai to their next objective, Nanking. Nanking fell, after a bitter struggle, on 12 December 1937, and the Chinese retreated to the west. They made a last stand at Hankow, but this had to be evacuated in October 1938.

The Chinese Retreat 1938

After the fall of Hankow, Chiang retreated to Chungking, a small town high in the western mountains, which was to remain his headquarters for the rest of the war. Hundreds of thousands of Chinese followed the army, taking anything they could carry. Factories were stripped of machinery, which was carried on men's backs, and by mule and horse, along the narrow mountainous roads. The Hankow power plant, including its eighteen ton turbine, was removed in this way and installed in the new little capital. The staff and students of ninety-four colleges and universities deserted their buildings in the east and joined the migration to the mountains.

The Japanese did not pursue them. The tracks were unsuitable for their motorized columns and, in any case, they reckoned the Chinese resistance would shortly crumble. They held all the plains from Manchuria down to the Yangtse and all the coastal ports. The only route to any coast open to Chiang was along the Burma Road to Mandalay and then by rail to south Burma.

Nor was Chiang in any hurry to fight back. His aim was, he said, to 'trade space for time'. In other words, by evacuating eastern China, to keep his army intact and force on the Japanese a lengthy occupation which would eventually weaken them. Then he would counter-attack.

For six years, from 1938 to 1944, he maintained this position. The border between the Japanese-occupied zone and free China was a fifty mile wide strip, mostly cleared of buildings and bridges by the Chinese as they retreated. The

Officers of the victorious Japanese army lecturing to the people
of a captured Chinese town

few towns in this area were the scene of bitter fighting between
the two armies. Changsha changed hands twice in the early
part of the war. The Japanese made several attempts to pene-
trate Chinese held territory but on each occasion they were
repulsed by the Chinese taking advantage of the mountainous
countryside.

Chiang made no effort to launch a major offensive against
the Japanese. Yet, in 1941, there seemed a chance that the
situation would change in his favour. For the first time in the
ten years since the conquest of Manchuria he had allies in the
struggle with Japan.

The Second World War

In 1941 Japan attacked the U.S. naval base at Pearl Harbour
and brought America into the Second World War. China's
war against Japan became part of a very much larger conflict which ranged over the Pacific Ocean and as far west as
Burma. China automatically became the ally of America and
Britain.

The Americans sent General Joseph Stilwell to Chungking,
to arrange for co-operation between Chinese and American

forces in the land war against the Japanese.

At first the struggle went in Japan's favour. She conquered Burma and closed the Burma Road, Chiang's last link with the outside world. The Americans came to his aid with an airlift from north India. Supplies were flown over 'the hump' (the Himalayas) in terrible conditions and with great loss of lives and machines. Unarmed cargo planes flew across six hundred miles of uncharted mountains and jungle at 20,000 feet. They overcame Japanese fighter attacks, tropical monsoons and icing at high altitudes, to bring up to 80,000 tons of equipment each month.

Stilwell hoped for a counter-offensive to drive the Japanese land forces from Burma, but he found Chiang unwilling to co-operate. His only interest seemed to be in getting ever-increasing amounts of American supplies flown over the hump. Stilwell blamed him for encouraging a defeatist spirit amongst his officers:

'Chiang Kai-shek has said on many occasions that a Chinese division did not have the fire-power of a Jap regiment, and that three Chinese divisions were not a match for one Jap division. Naturally his commanders eagerly accepted this statement as full excuse for running away.'

'He was going to trade space for time, a very catchy way

General Stilwell with one of Chiang's generals

of saying he would never attack.'

The trouble wasn't just that Chiang lacked any fighting spirit; his whole army was rotting. War correspondents were horrified at its condition. Disease was everywhere; it was estimated that ten per cent of the soldiers suffered from tuberculosis. Their rations were miserable and entirely lacking in vitamins, so that you found soldiers with gaping raw sores which dripped pus on to the ground. There were almost no doctors or military hospitals and injured men died from gangrene in their thousands.

Most of the officers were brutal and corrupt. Men were beaten and shot for minor offences. Commanders drew the pay for the full ten thousand in a division when it had, in fact, shrunk to six thousand and, in some cases, as low as two thousand.

After their brave stand in Shanghai and Nanking in 1938, Chiang's armies took practically no active part in the war. By 1944 they were weak, dispirited, short of equipment and waiting for the allies to defeat Japan for them.

Meanwhile the Red Army had shown a very different spirit.

The Red Army

At the beginning of the war Mao realized that it would last a long time and would give him the opportunity to seize the leadership of China from Chiang. He forecast correctly that the Kuomintang forces would rot through inactivity, and that Chiang's prestige would fall when he failed to make a counter-attack against the Japanese. The Red Army, on the other hand, was trained in guerrilla warfare and capable of carrying the war into the heart of the Japanese occupied area.

The guerrilla fighting was on a much larger scale than it had been in the Kiangsi-Hunan Soviet. Before the end of the war the Red Army had grown to over a million men. Yet it rarely operated as a large force. Bands of three to four hundred men stole through the occupied area alone, keeping in touch with their bases by wireless. If a weak Japanese position was spotted, radio messages could bring together a force of twenty thousand, which would attack and then disperse in small units. The Japanese never managed to crack the Communist wireless code which made these operations possible.

A company of Red soldiers carrying cannon made from hollowed wood

They tried to stop the guerrillas with their 'prisoner's cage tactic'. The occupied area was divided by wide trenches into blocks roughly ten miles square. After two years the length of the trenches was six times that of the Great Wall. Inside the squares the Japanese hoped to trap the guerrillas, but they very rarely did so. The smallness of the Communist bands made it possible for them to slip past sentries in the trenches, usually into a square which the Japanese had just left.

The Reds taught the people of occupied China to join in this game of hide and seek. A militia force of two million peasants was set up. Trained by Red Army instructors they were responsible for the defence of their own villages. The Japanese especially feared their mines:

'Anything within sight is likely to be mined. And in some districts almost everything is. A basket left in the middle of the road, a plowshare in the field, a paper-wrapped parcel by the wayside—all these things may be mined. A road rut is dug out, a mine is carefully buried, and an old auto tire is rolled lightly over the dusty surface. After a few Jap trucks are blown up in this way, Jap drivers will bump along the surfaces between the ruts—which are also mined.'

The peasants' children were enrolled as Red Army Children to act as messengers and scouts. When they warned of the

Red guerrilla soldiers plant a home-made land-mine in the path to be taken by Japanese troops

approach of Japanese troops, the militia would organize an 'Emptying the House and Clearing up the Field' operation. All furniture, food, stores and cattle would be moved or buried and the people would evacuate their village. Japanese patrols would enter to find it deserted and silent, apart from the sudden explosion of a land-mine or crack of a sniper's bullet.

The Liberated Areas

The districts where the Red Army was in touch with the villagers were known by the Communists as the liberated areas. By the end of the war they covered nine-tenths of the zone occupied by the Japanese. There were nearly one hundred and forty million Chinese in this area and the Japanese could not control them all directly. Consequently, the Communists were able to set up village councils which operated except when Japanese patrols came by.

Through these village councils they carried out the land programme that Mao had started in the Border Region. Every peasant was given land, and rents were reduced to a reasonable level. To avoid the charge of interference, it was a rule that only one-third of a village council should be Communist. Nevertheless, everyone knew that it was the Communists who had brought land reform to the villages, just as everyone saw that it was the Communists who were carrying on the fight against the Japanese.

This was the impression that Mao had intended to create. He knew that the Red Army had not the strength to meet the Japanese in an open pitched battle, any more than had the Kuomintang. But the guerrilla fight had given the Communists a valuable opportunity for propaganda. They described the Kuomintang as the corrupt landlords' party, which had run away from the Japanese; and compared it with the Communists, the party of the peasants, which had stood shoulder to shoulder with the people against the aggressors and still found time to correct age-old evils.

Mao waited confidently for the end of the war.

16   Communist Victory

The Race to the Japanese

In May 1945 Germany surrendered and the war in Europe was over. Britain and America were now able to transfer all their war effort to the task of defeating Japan, and Russia agreed to join them. Victory was hastened, at a terrible cost, when atom bombs were dropped on Hiroshima and Nagasaki on 6 and 9 August. On 14 August Japan surrendered.

The race was on. Mao's orders came over the radio from Yenan. The Communists were to move forward and accept the surrender of Japanese troops in east China and Manchuria. From Chungking, Chiang broadcast an order to the Communists to make no contact with the enemy. The Japanese must only surrender to government troops, he said. The Red Army ignored Chiang and began to take over the Japanese garrisons. They were in the front line; the government troops were hundreds of miles to the rear.

Chiang called on the Americans. He was the official head of an allied government and they were bound to meet his wishes. Half a million Kuomintang troops were carried to the Japanese positions in U.S. aircraft, and American marines took over the Peking-Manchuria railway on Chiang's behalf.

The result of these manoeuvres was that the Japanese occupied towns were surrendered to Kuomintang forces, but nearly all the countryside north of the Yangtse was taken over by the Red Army. There were clashes between the two armies and a major civil war seemed inevitable when the Americans stepped in.

General Marshall's Peace Mission

President Truman sent General Marshall to China with instructions to bring the two sides together for talks. Marshall hoped that he would be able to persuade both Mao and Chiang to co-operate in a coalition government.

He persuaded Mao to fly to Chungking for a meeting with Chiang, but this simply showed that agreement was impossible. Mao demanded sufficient share of the government to allow communism to continue to grow. Chiang was determined to keep full control of the country to prevent the spread of communism and the land reform movement started by the Reds.

After trying for a year, General Marshall flew back to New York and reported that there was nothing that could prevent civil war.

The Civil War

The war broke out in earnest in 1947. The Kuomintang was in control of all China south of the Yangtse, and most of the cities in the north and Manchuria. The only link between the scattered armies of the Kuomintang was by air, because the Communists held the roads and railways.

If Chiang was to win the war it was essential to clear one region of Communists, so that his troops had room to mass into a large enough force to open an offensive. He might have succeeded in doing this if he had tried to capture only one district in 1947. Instead he attacked in three different directions; towards Shantung, Yenan and Manchuria. Only in Yenan was he successful, and then only because the Communists had decided that the area was of little value, and were prepared to give it up.

While Chiang's forces were marching on their three fruitless campaigns, the Red Army slipped past them to the south and established a base in the Tapeh mountains. From here they controlled the route north from the Yangtse, and also threatened the Yangtse valley itself. They had turned the tables on Chiang and the end was in sight.

In 1948 it was their turn to go on the offensive, with rapid success. By January 1949 every city north of the Yangtse was in their hands. The campaign was more of a triumphant procession than a fight. Many cities surrendered without a shot being fired. Officers and men deserted in their thousands to the Red Army. It was not so much a victory for the Communists as a complete collapse of the Kuomintang.

The Kuomintang Collapse

In 1948 and 1949 a widespread wave of disgust with the Kuomintang swept China. A general who deserted with his army to the Communists told an American reporter how his experience at Chungking turned him against Chiang:

'I was disgusted by what I saw. No government office was doing anything. All the officials were just waiting for Chiang Kai-shek's orders. Everyone was grafting. A needle factory owner invited me to dinner and told me that he had to pay the Special Service agents of Chiang Kai-shek one hundred thousand dollars for every worker in his factory so they would not be conscripted. I was sick.'

Students and young people generally welcomed the Communists, because they were sickened with the brutality and corruption of Chiang's forces:

'I shall never forget the American girl who had volunteered to take care of some of the orphans. UNRRA had sent her supplies of food for them, but Chiang's officers prevented her from getting the food. Many of the children had died while the food that would have saved them was being sold out of a warehouse around the corner. "This is enough to make a Communist out of me", she had written.'

Communist propaganda assisted the Kuomintang collapse. Slogans were aimed at Chiang's use of American aid in the fight against his own countrymen: 'We did not want to be Japanese slaves: we don't want to be American slaves.'

The Communists were still careful to present themselves as moderate men who would bring no harm to non-communists. They captured Peking without a battle after broadcasting a promise to the people:

'People's lives and property will be protected. Keep order and don't listen to rumours. Looting and killing are strictly forbidden.

'Chinese individual commercial and industrial property will be protected. Private factories, banks etc., will not be touched and can continue operating.'

A writer described how they kept their word:

'After the fall of Peking the trembling deputy manager of a mint was visited by a communist official. Expecting the worst he took him to the plant. There he gave the place a quick once-over, asked a number of questions about organization, production, methods and wages and then turned to the deputy manager. "You seem to know what you're doing. You're in charge", he said.'

Reports that the Communists were not taking over businesses, and not harming businessmen, led many of them to break their twenty-year-old support of the Kuomintang and go over to the Communists.

Ordinary people in the streets were also impressed with Communist behaviour:

'Several times I saw a soldier approaching a knot of bystanders, . . . and proffering his paper with a polite bow and a wide smile, ask for directions to the street and house number his group were seeking. These must have been some of the first occasions in Tientsin's history of uniformed soldiers using all the forms of Chinese courtesy to ordinary civilians. On the civilians, at first astounded, and in the end mightily pleased, the effect was enormous.'

The Last Stages

Chiang's loss of support was so overwhelming that he had no choice but to surrender or flee the mainland. He chose the latter course. Communist forces crossed the Yangtse in April 1949 and the remnants of the Kuomintang fled southwards before them, and crossed to safety on the island of Formosa.

On 1 October 1949 Chairman Mao Tse-tung announced the foundation of the People's Republic of China. In Formosa, Chiang might have been calculating that it was just twenty-two years since he had so nearly annihilated the Chinese Communist Party at Shanghai.

17 Making China Communist

The first of October 1949 was a great day in the lives of Mao Tse-tung, Chou En-lai and the other Chinese Communist leaders. They emerged from twenty-two years in hiding and stood together on the top of the Gate of Heavenly Peace in Peking. There Mao announced to the entire world the setting up of the People's Republic of China, and then stood watching as the Red victory procession passed below. There were Red Army soldiers with their captured American weapons, peasant guerrillas with their home-made bombs, political workers and medical staff from the guerrilla forces, and young children who had guarded the entrance to liberated villages. For several hours the triumphant march continued; a living sign that new times had come to China.

Yet the Communist leaders knew that they were faced with dangers from every side. There were the Kuomintang forces in Formosa, who might at any time be helped by an anti-communist foreign power to strike back at the Reds. Many landlords and businessmen in China feared for their property, and their own safety, and might be tempted to join a 'counter-revolution'. Most serious of all was the ruin caused by twelve years of war. Industry was producing little more than half its pre-war output; food supplies were down to about three-quarters the pre-war level. Roads, railways, bridges and water-works had all suffered from damage and neglect. Shortages of every kind had led to a steep rise in prices, while Kuomintang mismanagement had resulted in a drastic fall in the value of money. You needed a small suitcase of banknotes to buy a new coat.

These were just the conditions which could lead to revolts

Mao proclaiming the People's Republic of China, 1 October
1949

against the new leadership and perhaps encourage unfriendly
powers to step in. It took three years of firm, and often harsh,
action to repair the damage of war and to establish firm
Communist control over the whole country.

The Control of Industry

The new government began by seizing control of all the large
wholesale trading organizations. By buying and selling goods
at fixed low rates, the new state trading companies stopped the
crazy rise in prices. Most companies making heavy industrial
goods were nationalized, too, although their owners were
often kept on as managers. Heavy industry was allowed the
greatest share of the rationed raw materials and was encouraged to build new plant and equipment. By 1952 pro-

duction of basic goods—coal, iron, steel and cement—was as high as the pre-war level.

Private banks were closed down and replaced by a State Bank, which could control the way the country developed by lending money only for new schemes approved by the government. Soldiers from the Red Army were set to work repairing the damaged railway lines and rebuilding roads and bridges. As soon as this work was completed, plans for building several thousand miles of new railway lines were drawn up.

By 1952 the government was ready to begin a large-scale industrial revolution, which would eventually make China into as rich and powerful a nation as Russia or the U.S.A. It was ready for the first of the Five Year Plans.

Land Reform

Sun Yat-sen had said that the most important task for a revolutionary government would be to give land to the tiller. The Communists had already begun to do this in the parts of China they had liberated before 1949. Early in 1950, the Agrarian Reform Law laid down that all land should be taken from landlords and transferred to the poor peasants in each village.

Land Reform was intended to do more than solve the problem of village poverty. It was a way of eliminating the landlords, who were the bitterest and most dangerous enemies of the new government, and a means of enrolling the support of the great mass of the peasants.

The method used was to encourage the peasants to carry out the reforms themselves in their own villages. Party cadres saw that the law was carried out throughout the country. They needed considerable patience, as the cadre, Ching, explained to an English journalist:

'So the first thing to do is to find out exactly who's who in the village and how the village works: who profits, who suffers. You generally choose to live with the poorest peasant you can find and you live with him—not eating or sleeping any better than he does. You do that until he sees you really mean it—until he gives you his confidence.'

Having won his confidence, Ching then formed a study group among the poorer peasants. Meetings were held to study ways of improving village life; and here the idea of land reform was first mentioned. But the peasants were not told that they had the right by law to seize the land of the rich; it was important that they should decide themselves to overthrow the landlords. So the next stage in the carefully thought-out campaign was the 'accusation meeting' or the 'speak bitter'.

Here bold peasants stood up and spoke of the wrongs they had suffered at the hands of the landlords; reminding their fellows of times they had been cheated out of land, of excessive rents, of how landlords had used force to seize land which was not rightfully theirs. Many peasants were timid and reluctant at first 'for fear we'd go away and the landlords would punish them for what we'd said'. But Ching was always in the background, encouraging even the most timid to stand up and 'speak bitter'.

For the landlords, compelled to face their angry accusers, it was a frightening and bewildering experience:

'Sometimes I was alone and the people would be shouting at me all the things they thought I had done wrong; sometimes they would have several of us at these meetings and the crowd would then be larger. . . . The people were sometimes very angry. I didn't understand any of it at first; I didn't know they had any special grievance against me. They then added up all the money they thought I owed them, so they said that the land I owned was really theirs now, for they had worked for years for too little.'

When the peasants had the courage to demand the confiscation of the landlords' property, they turned to the cadres for help in arranging its redistribution. Everyone in the village was classified into one of four groups: poor peasant, middle peasant, rich peasant and landlord. The landlord lost all his land, which was divided amongst the poor and middle peasants. The rich peasants kept their land, as the Communists did not want to make enemies of anyone but the landlords at this stage.

What of the landlords? Those whose past injustice had not been too great were allowed to stay in the village and were given the opportunity to work and be treated like the other villagers. But if the 'speak bitter' meetings had revealed cases

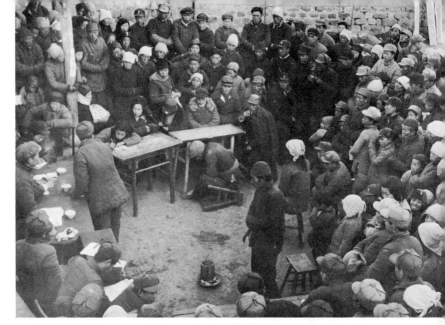
A People's Court

of very harsh treatment, they were brought before a 'people's court'. The whole village attended an open air meeting to accuse them of their crimes. The most damaging was to have been a supporter of the Kuomintang or to have collaborated with the Japanese. Some of them were sent to forced labour camps, but for the majority the sentence was death. Scores of thousands of landlords met their death during the Land Reform Campaign.

By 1952 Land Reform had been completed in every village in China, and a firm foundation had been laid for future progress along the path to communism. Each village contained a large number of peasants who had been poor or landless and who now had some land to cultivate. The Communists were able to count on their loyalty when they later introduced even more sweeping changes in village life.

Ruling by Persuasion

Between 1949 and 1952 the membership of the Communist Party rose from three million to five million. Most of the new members were drawn from workers in the towns, where previously the Party had been at its weakest. To be a Party member was looked upon as a privilege and only those who were prepared to give up their lives completely to the Party were allowed to join it.

The Party members were not the only tool used by the government to carry out its aim of establishing a firm grip on the country. All newspapers and books were brought under government control, so it was impossible to read criticisms of the Communists. The newspapers were often used to begin campaigns for new policies. Wherever possible the Communists preferred to use a mass propaganda campaign rather than direct force to get their way. This had happened in the case of Land Reform; it was also used to bring about the nationalization of light industry in 1952. Instead of simply taking over the industry, the government launched the 'Five-anti' campaign. Mass meetings, newspaper articles and posters all played their part in attacking the five crimes of bribery, tax dodging, fraud, theft of State property and revealing state economic plans. Keen Party members would report businessmen for one of these crimes. Thousands were arrested, tried and fined so heavily that they could no longer carry on their businesses and had to hand them over to the state.

How much cruelty and violence was used in setting up Communist control in China? No one knows the complete

Political processions are a common sight in Communist China. Here students march with banners showing Mao Tse-tung and Chu Teh, the Commander-in-Chief of the Red Army which defeated Chiang

answer. Certainly, in the first years, many thousands of land-lords and others were considered to be the enemies of communism, and were executed on the orders of the people's courts. But the Communist leadership gave orders for a halt to the killings. It preferred, in Mao's words, 'to allow them to live and remould themselves through labour into new people'.

'Remoulding through labour' was often a grim experience. The convicted men were sent to work on a new railway or irrigation works; or they were sent to prisons which were equipped with industrial machinery. Months and years of manual labour were only part of the remoulding. It was accompanied by long sessions of political study and discussion, to show the prisoners the error of their past way of life. As landlords, as employers, or as supporters of the Kuomintang, they had been guilty of crimes against the people. The prisoners were expected to practise 'Self criticism', to be able to stand up and show that they understood how their past actions had been wrong and their old ideas incorrect. The pressure of the ceaseless lectures and explanations on men already exhausted by long hours of unfamiliar work must have been almost unbearable.

Not all remoulding was carried out under such punishing conditions. Milder forms were used on groups of men who were not actually Kuomintang supporters or criminals, but simply slow in giving whole-hearted support to the Communists. Many university teachers, for instance, were reluctant to base their teaching on the theories of Karl Marx. They also tended to think of themselves as a separate class, apart from the great mass of uneducated people. So they were sent for a year to live and work with peasants or factory workers. Many of them had never known such people before and they were forced to learn, as Mao put it, that the people with farm dung on their legs were the backbone of China.

Missionaries and Merchants

The Communists also turned their skill in persuasion on the thousands of men and women from the Western 'imperialist' nations who were still in China in 1949. Those European trading companies which were still operating soon found themselves faced with increased taxes and demands that they should pay higher wages to their employees. It was made clear that they would be squeezed into bankruptcy in a very short time. Most of them took the hint, handed over their warehouses, factories and offices to the government and brought their European employees home.

In 1949 there were about nine thousand missionaries, Protestant and Catholic, in China. Their work was brought to an end by the 'Three-self Movement' which was launched in 1952. Party propaganda persuaded the Chinese Christians that they should run their churches themselves, pay for their upkeep without asking for foreign help and use only Chinese preachers. The 'Three-self' campaign was a strong hint to the foreign missionaries that they were no longer welcome. Most of them left as soon as possible, so that their Chinese congregations could not be accused of collaborating with representatives of unfriendly foreign powers.

18 Industry and Agriculture

From Mutual Aid to Communes

To feed China's growing population it was essential that food supplies should increase every year. For this larger farms and up-to-date methods were necessary. The Communists feared that, if they delayed changes, the peasants would become too attached to their newly won holdings. So, the year after land reform was completed, the cadres began to suggest that the villagers form themselves into 'mutual aid teams'. Peasants kept their own land, but pooled animals, equipment and their labour, in teams of ten or so families.

The result was larger and healthier crops, and this success made most of the peasants look favourably on the next Communist scheme, co-operative farming. Several mutual-aid teams were joined together, and all their land was then sown and harvested as a single operation. A committee decided on the most suitable crops, and was responsible for selling them. The profits were divided among the co-operative members, according to the amount of land they had contributed and the hours of work they had put in.

On the whole, the co-operatives satisfied the peasants, who found that their crops improved further, and that they were able to eat a little better. It took much more persuasion to get them to accept the higher-grade co-operative, or collective farm. On the collectives all private ownership of land was abolished, and the peasants were paid according only to the number of hours work they performed. Not surprisingly, many peasants resisted collectivization, which made them little better than farm labourers, only four or five years after they had been given their own land.

The government overcame the opposition by giving way to some of the peasants' criticisms. The cadres who ran the collectives were reprimanded for 'commandism', giving too many orders and not listening to complaints. The huge labour teams were broken up into small groups who were allowed to arrange their own work, provided it fitted into the plan for the whole collective. Each peasant was given enough private land to grow vegetables and keep pigs and hens. By such concessions, the government was able to persuade the peasants throughout the country to agree to collectivization by 1957.

Then, in August 1958, Chinese newspapers carried a report of a new experiment in the countryside. Twenty-seven collectives in Honan had joined together to form the Sputnik Commune, which had a total population of forty-three thousand people. The idea was praised by government leaders, and a country-wide campaign to form communes was launched by the Communist Party. By the end of the year, nearly every peasant in China had been included in one of twenty-six thousand communes.

The Communes

The agricultural work of a commune is run in very much the same way as in collective farming. What is new is that the teams do not only farm; they are often called upon to help with some large building project decided on by the commune committee. Roads, schools, hospitals and old people's homes are built. Nearly every commune has undertaken irrigation and water-storage schemes. The commune can draw on a large number of workers, who can make up for the acute shortage of machinery by their very numbers. It is still a common sight to see dams and reservoirs being built by peasants using nothing more than shovels and baskets to move away earth.

Another advantage is that the commune can develop small industries, which provide work during the times when there is no demand for agricultural labour. Machinery and equipment for the commune farms, and products for sale in the towns, are produced. These bring in cash, with which the commune can buy tractors, building materials or medical equipment. One commune, in 1964, had seven small enterprises: an experimental farm producing seed and saplings, a sugar refinery, a workshop where fertilizer was ground, a

Women members of a commune in the countryside of north China

small coal-mine, a farm implement factory, a workshop making fire-sand for iron castings and a quarry producing clay for pottery.

The communes now provide all the local public and welfare services. They are responsible for their own medical services, education and for the care of the old in the 'Homes of Respect for the Aged'. They provide canteens for workers' meals and nurseries for young children; very important services which make it possible for women to work in the communes' fields and factories.

At first they were criticized for breaking up family life. Some communes were reported to be issuing free food and clothing and even thinking of building large dormitories, so that the worker would have no private life nor would he have the responsibility of caring for his own family. Such schemes were discouraged by the government and soon abandoned. Nevertheless, the communes make it easy for the Communists to plan the lives of the Chinese people to a greater extent than a government can in any other country. They can persuade men and women to work only on schemes approved by the commune leaders, which are part of the national Five Year Plans. Periods of political study can be included in a normal

Pensioners from coal mines in a 'Home of Respect for the Aged'

working day. The commune leaders, who are loyal Party cadres, are soon aware of any grumblings against the government.

Most Chinese would probably agree that they have much

Much of China's agriculture still depends on age-old primitive techniques. Peasants working a tread-mill to irrigate the fields

to thank the communes for. Full employment, a share in the use of machinery and motor vehicles, sometimes supplies of electricity, all make life easier. The communes care for the very young and the old, and ease the burden of being a working mother. For such reasons they have been generally accepted, and will remain a feature of Chinese life for many years to come.

The First Five Year Plan

In 1952 China began the first of the Five Year Plans through which the government controls the future development of industry. Special emphasis was laid on food, heavy industry and mining, for China was a desperately poor country and could not think of producing any more than the bare minimum of 'consumer goods'. These are the products of light industry such as furniture, kitchen equipment or clothing, which are consumed by people and do not help in the making of other goods.

By the end of the first Plan, food production had gone up by a quarter, from 160 million tons to 200 million tons a year. Production had doubled for coal, cement and machine tools, trebled for oil and quadrupled for steel. The first Chinese built lorries had appeared in 1956, and the first oil-tanker and light aircraft in 1957. But production had been so extremely low at the beginning of the plan that these achievements still left her way behind the industrialized nations. Steel output was still only 5·3 million tons, compared with Britain's 20 million and the U.S.A.'s 100 million tons. Yet China had a population three times as great as that of the United States. A census taken in 1953 showed that there were 582,603,417 Chinese,[1] and that their numbers were growing by two per cent, or about 13 million each year. By 1962 there would be 700 million Chinese; an extra 120 million mouths to feed.

Such numbers, of course, could one day make China the greatest power on earth. Her leaders knew that Soviet Russia, the world's first communist state, had overcome similar difficulties and raised herself to be almost the equal of America in industrial strength. They, too, were determined to prove that communism was the road to wealth and power, and it was

[1] And approximately another ten million in Formosa.

131

decided that the next Five Year Plan should be the time of the 'Great Leap Forward'.

The Second Five Year Plan

The aims for even the first year of the second Plan were staggering. Steel was to double its output and food production was to rise by more than it had done over the previous five years. People outside China said that such increases were impossible. The Communists answered that it could be done by 'walking on two legs'.

What they meant was that the targets would be reached by using both new and old-fashioned methods of production. Steel, for instance, need not only be made in huge modern rolling mills; small quantities could be produced in hundreds of thousands of backyard furnaces. This was where the small industries set up by the communes could play their part. By establishing small factories throughout the countryside, China could become an important industrial nation without having to wait until new factories and new cities, to house industrial workers, were built.

The first year of the 'Great Leap Forward' was pleasing. Many targets were reached, though some mistakes were made. About three million tons of steel made in small furnaces were found to be of such poor quality that it was useless for anything but making small farm implements. However, it was the setback of the next three years which proved really disappointing. Food production between 1959 and 1961 fell back to the level of 1956. This was partly due to a succession of floods and droughts, as bad as anyone had ever known. The government admitted, too, that it had made the mistake of over-emphasizing industry at the expense of agriculture, and about twenty million people were returned from manufacturing to farming. To avoid famine, food was bought from abroad, mostly in the form of grain from Canada, Australia and South America.

Industry was dealt a sharp blow in these years by the withdrawal of Russian help in 1960. Under an agreement made in 1950, the Soviet Union had promised to help China with about two hundred projects for metal and chemical factories, aeronautical works and power stations. She loaned China the

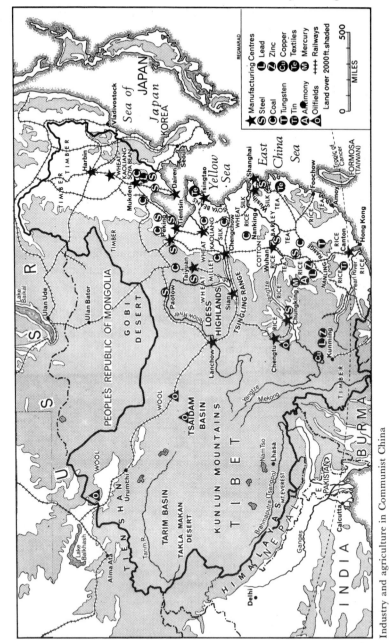

Industry and agriculture in Communist China

equipment for these and supplied hundreds of designers and technicians. By 1960 the two countries had quarrelled bitterly. All Russian aid was stopped and the technicians recalled home. China was left with a debt of about 700 million pounds which it took five years to pay off.

The Chinese leaders refused to admit that they were discouraged by these setbacks and still talked of the 'Great Leap Forward', which was continued by the third Five Year Plan which began in 1962.

China's New Industries

Although 'walking on two legs' has made a valuable contribution to China's industrial development, her aim of joining the world's great industrial nations still depends on her large-scale factories and mines. A widespread search for minerals has proved that the country is rich in natural resources. She has larger reserves of coal than any other country except the United States. Oil has been found in the north-west, and larger amounts are produced each year. The country is exceedingly rich in iron ore and in many rarer metals of crucial importance in modern industry, such as antimony, tin, tungsten and bauxite.

A cotton mill, state-owned, like all factories in China today

Steel rolling mill in Anshan, Manchuria

In 1949 the only heavy industry was in Manchuria, where coal, iron and steel works had been built by the Japanese. The Chinese have added new industries: machine tools, motor vehicles, aeroplanes, chemicals and electrical equipment. New districts are being developed as industrial centres, such as the areas around Peking and Tientsin. Three hundred miles to the south west of Peking, new iron and steel works have been built at Taiyuan and electrical, machine-tool and aeronautical works have grown around them. The towns of the Yangtse, developed by foreigners as ports and textile manufacturing centres, are now producing heavy industrial and electrical goods. The old cotton mills of the Yangtse have been modernized, and new mills built on the cotton fields in Honan. China is now the world's largest producer of cotton goods.

The spreading of industry spotlighted the weakness of China's transport system. The foreigners who built the first railways built them near the coast and in Manchuria. The Communists have begun the immense task of providing railway links with the new industries of the interior and with the oilfields of the north west. As motor vehicles are now being made, although in small quantities by European standards, new roads have to be built. Some of the longest have been made in the mountainous districts of the west, where railway building would be extremely difficult.

Yet, like most things in China, the transport system is a mixture of the old and new. Donkeys, mules, camels and hand-carts are still used for local transport. For long distances the rivers are still important, as they have been for thousands of years; but nowadays tugs and outboard motors are beginning to provide the power once supplied by sail or the muscles of men and animals.

What has been done in China since 1949 shows that, although it will be many years before she can match the industrial strength of Russia and America, she has laid a good foundation for progress to this goal. She is also training large numbers of scientists and technicians and spending a great amount on scientific research. In 1964 she became the fifth nation in the world to explode an atomic bomb.

China is taking the industrial lead in Asia. Already she is producing more than India, and is able to export machine tools and other goods to other Asian nations. In this way she is strengthening her claim to be the political leader of the underdeveloped world.

19 The Government of Communist China

People living in countries where there are several political parties regard the communist system of government as a dictatorship, because it allows the existence of only one political party. The communists, however, speak of their state as a 'People's Democracy', because members of the government at all levels are elected. The chief difference in the communist method is that really important decisions are made, not in the elected governing bodies, but in the private sessions of the Communist Party, which are open to only a small percentage of the people.

For local government the people of several villages or small towns are grouped together and called a *Hsiang*. (Today the people of one commune often make up a *Hsiang*.) They elect a *Hsiang* Congress. Several *Hsiangs* make up a *Hsien*, which is equivalent to a county or a large city. Each *Hsiang* Congress elects a few of its members to serve on the *Hsien* Congress. *Hsiens* are grouped into Provinces and each *Hsien* sends representatives to the Provincial Congress. From the Provincial Congresses, members are elected to the National People's Congress.

Each congress elects a council for the area it serves, and it is these councils which carry out the policies of the State Council, which is the nearest equivalent of our cabinet. It is headed by the Chairman of the People's Republic, and includes the men and women ministers who are responsible for the main government departments, such as Foreign Affairs, Health, Education and so on.

The congress system means that, in theory, there is an upward channel through which the government can learn of the feelings of the people. The Communists probably regard this as less important than the downward channel of the State Councils, which brings all parts of China under the direct orders of the State Council in Peking. In any case, actual

137

The real power lies with the Communist Party headed by its Chairman & members of the Politbureau

| Chairman of the Party / Politbureau / Central Committee | Party Provincial Congress | Party Hsien Congress | Local Committees of the Communist Party |

| Chairman of the Peoples' Republic / Prime Ministers & Ministers / State Council | Provincial Council | Hsien Council | Hsiang Council |

The Councils carry out the directions of the State Council

| National People's Congress | Provincial Congress | Hsien Congress | Hsiang Congress |

which choose the Councils

The People elect the Congresses

The Government of Communist China

power in China lies with the Communist Party. At every level of government the Party has a corresponding organization where the real decisions are made.

Party members do everything possible to influence elections, so that only people acceptable to the Party stand as candidates for the congresses and councils. A Communist Party secretary sits on each council and, at all levels, discussion in the congresses and councils takes place only after a policy has been thrashed out privately in a Party meeting. Thus it is the Communist Party, numbering only two per cent of the people, which really governs China.

The Communists try to avoid the charge of dictatorship. The cadres do act as the 'Party's eyes and ears among the masses', and report cases of discontent with a new law or a new political campaign. They also try to see that the candidates for election to the congresses and councils are acceptable to the people as well as to the Party. Cadres who have tried to set up local dictatorships have often been reprimanded by the Party leaders.

It is also important to remember that even the small place in government allowed to the ordinary Chinese is much greater than anything he was allowed under the Kuomintang or the Manchu Empire. At present, therefore, he is probably satisfied with the Communist government, but in years to come there will certainly be demands for a more representative system.

The National Minorities

The truly Chinese people, the race known as the Han Chinese, make up about ninety-four per cent of the population of the People's Republic. This leaves about forty million people who are non-Chinese. Most of these minorities live on the western and northern borders, in regions overrun by China at some point in her long history. Six and a half million Chuang occupy Western Kiangsi, there are nearly three million Buddhist people in Tibet and nearly four million Uighur people, who are Muslims, live in the huge province of Sinkiang.

The Chinese constitution allows these, and other minority peoples, the right to develop the use of their own language

A Turk from north-west China

and to follow their own religious faith. The provinces in which they live are known as Autonomous Regions and, although they are drawn in to the national government's plans for political and economic affairs, they are allowed to control their own education so that minority languages are taught. They use their own languages in the law-courts, in the congresses and on bank notes.

In addition to the Autonomous Regions which cover whole provinces, there are many smaller ones, which keep the minority language alive in *Hsiens* where the majority of the people are non-Chinese.

The Cultural Revolution

One-party government does not mean that China's leaders never disagree. When the Great Leap Forward failed, some of its supporters were dismissed. Even Mao was forced to resign as President of People's China although he kept the important position of Chairman of the Party. In August 1966 he began to make a come-back supported by Lin Piao who was Minister of Defence. They launched the Cultural Revolution, aimed at Party Officials who showed little enthusiasm for further struggles to build Communism. They were to be driven forward by the enthusiasm of the young people inspired by the thoughts of Chairman Mao.

Schools and Colleges were closed, young people were re-cruited into the Red Guards, and flocked to mass meetings in Peking. They were sent away to carry the Cultural Revolution throughout China. In every city Red Guards painted 'big character posters' with the thoughts of Mao, changed street names that seemed to them anti-communist, forced rickshaw passengers to change place with the men between the shafts. Some activities were uglier; men and women they considered 'enemies of the people' were mobbed.

The real point of the Cultural Revolution was seen when the Red Guards tried to take over the Party committees and trade unions. They were resisted by older party officials, and in towns such as Shanghai and Canton fierce fighting broke out. By early 1967 the Cultural Revolution was weakening China's industrial growth. Some peasants took the opportunity to leave the communes. A slowing down was called for in the spring but the disturbances went on for two years.

In the 1970s political life became quieter. One result of the Cultural Revolution was that the army was able to demand a more important place in the government. The wilder figures had disappeared. Lin Piao was reported to have been discovered plotting to overthrow the government. According to the Chinese he was killed when the plane in which he was fleeing the country crashed. After the Great Leap Forward and the Cultural Revolution the Chinese leaders came to prefer steady development to attempts to rush forward by mobilising the masses.

20 China and the World – I

The Alliance with Russia

When the Communists gained control of China, the rest of the world waited anxiously to see what their attitude towards Russia would be. In 1949 the 'Cold War' between Communist and non-Communist nations was uppermost in everyone's thoughts. In the previous year Communists had seized power in Czechoslovakia, the last of the eastern European countries to come under Communist control and join the 'bloc' of nations who invariably followed the lead of Soviet Russia. In April 1949 the countries of Western Europe and North America had replied by setting up the North Atlantic Treaty Organization. Its policy of 'containment', or holding back the spread of communism, would have much less chance of success if Russia gained a huge new ally.

Since the Shanghai Massacres in 1927 there had been no contact between the Chinese Communists and Russian Communists who never believed that Mao's peasant communism could succeed. Nevertheless, Russia was the only country likely to support China in her plan to annihilate the last remnants of the Kuomintang forces. In February 1950 Mao went to Moscow to sign a treaty of friendship. In the following months, troops, ships and aircraft were assembled on the south coast ready for an autumn attack on Formosa. But it was never launched, for, on 25 June 1950, the Korean War broke out.

The Russians were fully aware that fighting was about to break out, but they gave no warning to the Chinese, although they must have known that they would almost certainly become involved in the war. Indeed, within twelve months, China was at war, not with the weakened forces of Chiang, but the combined armies of fifteen nations.

The Korean War 1950–53

Korea had been in the hands of Japan since 1910. After the Japanese surrender in 1945, Russian forces had occupied the north and Americans the south. Both powers had agreed to leave as soon as the Koreans had elected a government. But this proved difficult. Korean politics were confused and the people had little experience of democracy. The Americans feared that the growing Korean Communist Party would be encouraged by the Russians to seize power and wanted to declare communism illegal. The Russians countered by demanding that some of the right wing parties be banned. Soon they gave up all pretence of trying to reach an agreement and set up a communist government in the north with-

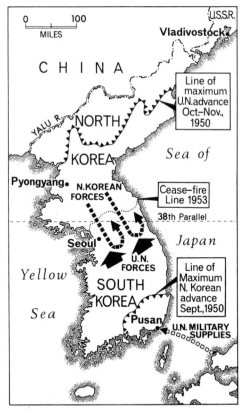

The Korean War

out holding elections. The Americans were then able to organize elections, but only in the south. These resulted in a government headed by Syngman Rhee which, unfortunately, soon became little more than a dictatorship.

In 1948–9 both powers withdrew their forces, leaving behind a United Nations Commission to try to bring the two halves of the country together. But both north and south now seemed determined to reunite Korea by force. The thirty-eighth parallel which divided them was the scene of constant clashes and raids by both sides. On 25 June the north Koreans crossed the parallel in an all-out effort to overrun the south. This was no mere raid. The north was using troops trained and equipped by the Russians. They were armed with tanks and supported by a sea landing.

It was a clear case of aggression, prompted by Russia, and possibly the forerunner of communist expansion into Asia similar to their advance into Europe. The United Nations Security Council declared north Korea the aggressors and called upon member nations to aid the south. The United States, anxious to prevent the spread of communism, answered the call the next day. She was able to transfer troops from General MacArthur's army of occupation in Japan. These were later joined by smaller forces from fifteen other nations, who all fought under MacArthur's command.

The American President, Harry Truman, also announced that the U.S. Seventh Fleet would keep Formosa neutral during the fighting in Korea. As Chiang Kai-shek was in no position to attack the mainland, this was, in effect, a warning to the Communist Chinese that America would prevent them from attacking Formosa. A wave of bitter anti-American feeling was whipped up by the Communist government, and grew as the United Nations forces in Korea pushed back the north's armies.

At first it had been the north Koreans who were successful. The south, together with the first U.N. troops, had been forced almost to the southernmost tip of the country. Then, at the end of September, the situation was dramatically reversed. A U.N. counter-attack, supported by a landing at the port of Seoul, drove the invaders back to the thirty-eighth parallel. Chou En-lai, then China's foreign secretary, warned the Americans that if their forces crossed the parallel, China would aid the north Koreans. The Americans, however, pressed on. A week later the Chinese, claiming that the Americans were now themselves aggressors, sent their first troops into Korea.

At first they shared the fate of the north Korean army, which was pushed further and further north until it had reached the Yalu river, the boundary between China and Korea. Then further Chinese reinforcements turned the tide. Two hundred thousand took part in the counter-attack which forced the United Nations back to the parallel by Spring 1951.

This stage of the war was accompanied by a bitter campaign of hatred aimed at America. Throughout China the 'Aid Korea; resist America' campaign was carried into every street. Posters showed the brutal American soldier torturing the innocent Korean citizen and the Americans were accused of using germ warfare. Collections were made to raise funds to help send more and more Chinese 'volunteer' soldiers to aid the Koreans.

The Americans were no less bitter about the Chinese, who had thwarted them of victory. General MacArthur wanted to bomb China itself, and for a time it looked as if a third world war might break out. Fortunately President Truman saw this risk and decided that the war must not be allowed to spread beyond Korea. He dismissed MacArthur, who had let his

Communist delegates arrive at Panmumjom for peace talks which, after many delays, ended the fighting in Korea

disagreement with the President become public.

Shortly afterwards, with both sides still fighting near the parallel, negotiations for a cease-fire began. They lasted for two years, for neither side wanted to give way and there was disagreement about the return of prisoners. Finally a cease-fire was signed in July 1953.

The war had not solved any of Korea's problems. The country remains divided at the cease-fire line. One in every ten Koreans had been killed and both north and south were devastated. Both America and China, however, claimed a victory. The Chinese government told the people that the war had proved that the Americans were only a 'paper tiger'. The United States government claimed that they had checked the spread of communism in Asia. Both realized that this was only the beginning of a struggle which would go on for many years. Many of China's neighbours were countries troubled by grave unrest and disorder, and all of them were desperately poor. China announced her sympathy with those neighbours who were fighting to free themselves from European colonial government. America felt that China might herself dominate these countries after they had won independence.

So peace did not follow the Korean armistice; the crisis centres merely shifted to two new areas, Formosa and Indo-China.

One consequence of the Korean war was the strengthening of the Red Army, which became the world's largest land force

21   Formosa and Indo-China

Formosa

In 1945 the people of Formosa had greeted with joy the Kuomintang officials who were sent to rule the island when the Japanese withdrew. They were soon shocked by the corruption of these officials, who seized food supplies and the private property of Formosans for themselves. So bad was their government that, in two years, the island's industry had collapsed completely, plague and cholera had broken out for the first time in thirty years, and food prices had risen by seven times. In 1947 a revolt broke out against the Kuomintang. It began when Formosans, demonstrating against the murder of a poor cigarette seller by the Kuomintang police, were fired on by machine guns. Widespread rioting followed and was put down with horrible brutality, 10,000 Formosans being killed by the Kuomintang troops.

When Chiang brought his 300,000 troops to the island in 1949 he cannot have been very welcome. It is almost certain that Formosa would have been seized by the Communists in 1950, for, up to the outbreak of the Korean war, the Americans had been refusing Chiang's demands for help. After the Korean cease-fire, however, they not only continued to protect Formosa with their Seventh Fleet, but gave Chiang vast amounts of military aid. This was not intended merely for defence, but to help the Nationalists, as the Kuomintang were called, to free China from Communist control.

The risk that an attack on Formosa would lead to war against America did not stop the Chinese from taking up a threatening attitude. In 1954–5 Formosa and the two offshore islands, Quemoy and Matsu, were shelled from the mainland and a major war seemed likely. The Communists did not, however, launch the expected full-scale attack. In 1958, the

Nationalist troops parading in Formosa

shelling was renewed after the Americans had built missile bases for Chiang in Formosa. After several tense weeks, the Americans prudently forced Chiang to withdraw most of his forces from the offshore islands. He was also told that America would not now help him in the reconquest of China, but would merely defend him against Communist attack.

Since 1958 the likelihood of war over Formosa has decreased. As Communist China's strength has grown, there is clearly no hope of a successful attack on the mainland by the Nationalists. With Chiang's death they may come to terms with the Communists.

Formosa, Peking and the U.N.

When the United Nations was set up after the Second World War, China was one of the five 'big powers' given a permanent seat on the Security Council. After 1949 the Communist government claimed that it ought to be admitted to the U.N., in place of the Nationalist government-in-exile of Chiang Kai-shek. All attempts to win admittance for Red China were voted down by members, led by the U.S.A., who looked on the Communists as rebels rather than a lawful government. In the 1960s, several states, including Britain and France, supported the Communist case. America changed her position as far as putting forward the Two Chinas policy, that both Peking and Formosa should be represented. By 1971 there was only a handful of support for this. A vote to replace Formosa by People's China was passed by more than the two-thirds majority which is needed under the United Nations' rules.

Indo-China

Japan had occupied the French colony of Indo-China during the Second World War. Their hold over the country had been challenged by a resistance movement known as the Vietminh. It was a communist movement whose leader, Ho Chi-minh, was a warm admirer of Mao Tse-tung and trained his peasant followers in the guerrilla tactics of the Red Army. After the Japanese surrender the Vietminh continued the fight for independence, this time against the French who intended to re-occupy their colony. The French took over the towns but never re-established control of the countryside, which was in the firm grip of the Vietminh.

The war against the French was still raging when the Chinese Communists came to power in 1949. They had no wish to see a European power successfully established across the border and sent aid to Ho Chi-minh. The Vietminh were allowed to enter China for periods of rest and training, and they were supplied with weapons, particularly with much-needed artillery. America gave two billion dollars worth of aid to the French. In this case, however, it was the Chinese aid which was more effective and which tipped the scales at Dien Bien Phu, where the final deciding battle between the French and the Vietminh was fought in 1954.

The French had deliberately invited a Vietminh attack on the fortress, believing that the guerrillas could not possibly bring up enough supplies for their front line troops and that the Vietminh had no heavy artillery. They were wrong on both counts. Ho Chi-minh's hold on the people was strong and no fewer than eighty thousand peasants wheeled bicycles through the jungle, carrying food and arms to the guerrilla fighters. And, of course, the Vietminh did have artillery: supplied by the Chinese. The result was utter defeat for the French after a heroic defence of the fort.

The defeat led to the French decision to withdraw. A conference at Geneva, in 1954, arranged for the creation of four independent states: Cambodia, Laos, South Vietnam and North Vietnam. Of these, only North Vietnam was given to Ho Chi-minh and his communist Vietminh. The other states came under the rule of noble or royal families.

S.E.A.T.O. and Neutralism

The Chinese looked on the Vietminh victory as a triumph. The Americans, on the other hand, were deeply alarmed about the spread of Communism in Asia. In 1953 they had given up half of Korea to Communism and, only a year later, half of Vietnam had gone the same way. President Eisenhower talked of South-East Asia falling to communism like a set of dominoes—once one country was knocked down all the others would fall. To prevent this, the Americans set up the South East Asia Treaty Organisation. S.E.A.T.O. was backed by America, France and Britain, but many Asian countries believed it was an attempt by white Western nations to rebuild their power in the East. Only Pakistan and Thailand joined.

Most other Asian nations preferred the policy which came to be known as neutralism. This meant they would support neither side in the struggle between the Western and Communist powers. A conference of twenty-nine African and Asian neutralist states was held at Bandung in 1955, and brought into being what is sometimes called the Afro-Asian Block. This is a group of states which often vote together at the United Nations. They are opposed to the old type of colonialism and also to 'neo-colonialism', by which they mean interference in their affairs by stronger powers who gain influence either through trade and business or by giving military help and advice.

China was quick to announce her sympathy with neutralism. Chou En-lai went to the Bandung conference to tell the Afro-Asian nations that China would not interfere in their affairs. Most of them, however, were wary of China, knowing that she would be pleased to see the Communist Parties in the neutralist countries seize power and make an alliance with her.

In 1965 their fears seemed to come true when there was an attempt to overthrow the government of Indonesia. The Indonesian Communist Party was involved in the revolt, which failed. The failure led to the fall of the neutralist President Sukarno and Indonesia was governed by the pro-western General Suharto, a vigorous anti-Communist.

Chou En-lai at the Bandung Conference

The Indonesian Communist Party was banned, its sympathisers were driven from government posts and many of its leaders massacred in violent anti-Communist riots encouraged by the government. The rioting also led to the deaths of hundreds of non-Communist Chinese in Indonesia.

In the 1970s, China made new attempts to find friends among her neighbours and her spokesmen began to talk of a world divided into three, the super powers, the other advanced states and the Third World. It was the Third World China hoped to lead and she increased her contacts with many countries in Africa and Asia, often by trading and by helping with their economic planning. Her task was made easier because, in the ten years between 1965 and 1975, the power of Britain and America in Asia was greatly weakened. Britain began to run down her bases and made it clear that she would not be able to defend the countries with whom she had defence arrangements. But the most dramatic change came in the rapid fall of American influence in Indo-China.

Indo-China in the Sixties and Seventies

Of the four states created in 1954, Cambodia became at first a neutralist state while both Laos and Cambodia accepted massive amounts of military help from the U.S.A. Both these countries had a succession of governments, most of them corrupt and unable to remedy the grinding poverty of their people. Partly for this reason, and partly due to help from Ho-Chi-minh's government in North Vietnam, Communism became a strong movement among the

China's southern neighbours

peasants. Civil wars broke out between Communist guerillas, supported by North Vietnam, and the governments of Laos and South Vietnam who received help from America. In 1970 the same pattern began in Cambodia. The neutralist president was forced to flee to China and war began between the pro-American government and a Communist army.

In 1964 the war in Vietnam had become a grave international problem. The Communist guerillas, the Vietcong, were steadily gaining control of more of the countryside. Arguing that this was a case of Communist aggression because the Vietcong were helped with supplies and re-inforcements from the north, the U.S.A. began to bomb North Vietnamese ships and military bases. In 1965 and 1966 they increased their already large and well-equipped forces in Vietnam.

The war became a controversial question. Critics of the American government argued that the Vietcong was a peasant political movement fighting a civil war and that the U.S.A. had no right to interfere. The U.S. government, however, argued that they were defending the South Vietnamese from aggression, and that the security of the whole of South-east Asia was at stake. The extent of the Peking government's involvement is not certainly known, but it gave only limited aid to the Vietcong, probably believing that their guerilla tactics would win in the end.

Opposition grew in the States. Politicians and voters questioned whether victory was possible. The use of rockets and napalm and heavy bombing of North Vietnamese towns severely damaged the U.S.'s reputation in the world. In 1968, President Johnson ordered the start of peace talks. They dragged on in Paris until the spring of 1973 when an armistice was signed. The Americans agreed to withdraw their armies, and the South Vietnamese government and the Communists were each to keep the territory they held at the cease-fire. The armistice suggested that north and south Vietnam would one day re-unite, but did not say how this was to happen.

It took place by force two years later. A combined Vietcong and North Vietnamese force opened a campaign against the South Vietnamese government. Gradually they seized the countryside and towns around Saigon. In April 1975 they entered the capital as the U.S.A. organised a huge evacuation by air and sea of American citizens and South Vietnamese who supported the old government. It was only a matter of weeks before the two other Indo-Chinese states fell into Communist hands. In Cambodia the government was driven out by the Communist Khmer Rouge which brought the neutralist president Sihanouk back from China. In Laos, the Pathet Lao set up a Communist government after seizing the country's capital.

As the U.S.A. began to lose her military power in South-east Asia she set out to improve relations with China. In 1971 President Nixon flew to Peking for talks with China's leaders, as did the British foreign secretary. The U.S. government allowed businessmen to trade with China. On October 25th, 1971, it voted for Communist China's membership of the United Nations. In 1975, after the fall of Indo-China to Communism, Mr. Kissinger, the American secretary of state, visited China.

22 China and the World – II

Tibet

Tibet, lying on a plateau fifteen thousand feet high to the east of the Himalayas, has only three million people. For centuries they have followed a form of the Buddhist faith and accepted the rule of their lamas, or priests, without question. The head of the state until 1959 was the Dalai Lama, whom the Tibetans believed to be the reincarnation of a god, the Lord of Mercy. When a Dalai Lama died, priests searched the countryside for a baby who showed signs of having been chosen by the Lord of Mercy for his next reincarnation. He was then taken away from his parents and trained in the duties of a Dalai Lama. At eighteen he took over the government from the priests and ruled Tibet from his palace in the capital, Lhasa, until his death.

China has always claimed suzerainty, or the right to supervise the government, in Tibet. During the Manchu period, however, she lacked the strength to exercise firm control over a country so far from Peking, and the Tibetans suffered little interference. The success of the Communists in 1949 altered this situation, for they were determined to re-establish Chinese control.

They entered Tibet in 1950 and set up a Tibetan government which, they said, could control internal affairs, provided that China controlled Tibet's foreign policy. The Dalai Lama was allowed to remain as head of the state, but in all matters of importance he was expected to take guidance from Chinese Communist officials in Lhasa.

They found Tibet a strange contrast to China, where land reform was going ahead and the feudal power of the landlords was being broken. It was the aim of the Communists to break the power of the priests and landlords, confiscate the wealth of the monasteries, and to persuade the mass of the people to accept that the Chinese brought the benefits of the modern world—roads, motor vehicles, medical services and education, all of which were sadly lacking in Tibet. The Tibetans, however, looked upon the Chinese as foreign conquerors, and they found it extremely difficult to win any co-operation. In the middle 1950s, a revolt against Chinese rule began amongst a wild tribe of Khambas, a Tibetan people living in China itself, and soon spread to Tibet. Priests led the resistance, which was put down with great severity by the Chinese. Very little of this was known to the outside world until the Dalai Lama escaped from Lhasa and fled to India. Here, he claimed that the Chinese had killed sixty-five thousand Tibetans, destroyed a thousand monasteries and attempted to destroy the Buddhist religion. Forty-three thousand Tibetans escaped with him and today live in India, many of them employed on road building schemes.

The Dalai Lama arrives in India

The Himalayan Border

China's claims to Indian territory

When the Chinese had overrun the whole of Tibet in 1959, they settled troops on the frontier with India. The true line of this frontier had never been agreed. The British, during their occupation of India, had drawn it at the Macmahon line, but China never signed any treaty agreeing to this. The Macmahon line runs along the crest of the Himalayas; the Chinese say the true boundary should run along the foot of the mountains. If this were so, they would gain about 32,000 square miles of Indian territory, the part usually known as the North-East Frontier Agency. Further west another area was in dispute, the plateau known as the Askai Chin. The Askai Chin had been included by the British in their maps of India; but again the Chinese had never agreed to this arrangement. No one had bothered much over the true ownership of such a barren area until the Chinese Communists seized Tibet. Then they found that the only route for a road from Tibet to the westernmost part of China, Sinkiang, was over the Askai Chin. The road was built between 1956 and 1958, the Chinese claiming that the Askai Chin really belonged to Tibet.

At the same time maps began to appear in Peking newspapers showing the disputed areas as Chinese. The Indians had to face the unpleasant fact that China was bent on seizing territory which was generally recognized as Indian. This was a shock, for she had always shown friendship to China. She had been one of the first nations to give official recognition to the Communist government and had acted as peacemaker, carrying messages between the Chinese and Americans, during the Korean peace negotiations. In 1954, the two governments had signed a declaration announcing their willingness to live side by side in a state of peaceful coexistence.

Now, Chinese replies to anxious Indian notes showed that they had no intention of withdrawing their claims to the Himalayan lands. Chinese troops appeared on the Indian side of the Macmahon line and there were skirmishes with Indian soldiers. Then, in 1962, the Chinese launched an attack which forced the Indians to retreat to the plains of north India.

The fighting then stopped and the Chinese withdrew to the Macmahon line, although they did not evacuate the Askai Chin, which they still hold. It looked as if they were not so much interested in winning new territory as in proving themselves to be the only Asian nation strong enough to interfere in a neighbour's affairs. India, a democratic country with a westernized parliamentary government, was China's most likely rival for the leadership of Asia.

This view of China's purpose in attacking India was confirmed in 1965 during the war between India and Pakistan over Kashmir. At the height of the conflict, China came forward with demands for the return of territory which, she claimed, had been illegally included in Sikkim, a state protected by India. These demands, too, were dropped, but China had made the point that she was a force to be reckoned with in Asian affairs. If she had pressed her claims, India would have been forced to fight a war on two fronts, against China in the north-east as well as Pakistan in the north-west.

The Quarrel with Russia

Observers noted that Russia gave no support to the Chinese attacks on India. By 1962 the friendship between the two countries had turned into bitter rivalry.

This was chiefly due to the new Russian approach to foreign affairs. Under the leadership of Mr Krushchev, Russia stopped being automatically opposed to America in everything she did. Krushchev knew that his country was developing quickly and drawing close to America in wealth and, more important, in military power. He began to suggest that, instead of opposing each other all over the globe, Russia and America could act better as joint world policemen. The Chinese still felt that America was the arch enemy, and that the world communist movement should resist her at all costs. They mocked at Krushchev for his 'soft' attitude towards the United States, particularly during the crisis of 1962 when he agreed to dismantle rocket bases that Russia had been supplying to Cuba.

Another cause for disagreement was that Russia had begun to supply underdeveloped non-communist countries with arms and economic help. Mao argued that many of the governments helped by Krushchev were *bourgeois*. He was, for instance, prepared to give aid to Nehru, a convinced anti-communist who would use these arms to defend the Indian border against Chinese attack.

Nuclear arms came into the argument. In 1963 Russia, Britain and the United States signed an agreement to carry out no further nuclear tests. The Russians must have signed knowing that the Chinese were building atomic bombs, and would want to test them soon. (In fact the first was exploded in north-west China in October 1964.)

The Chinese could not share the feeling of Krushchev, and some other Russian leaders, that the Cold War between East and West was expensive and wasteful. The Soviet Union had reached the stage where it was capable of producing the non-essential goods which would make life easier for the Russian people. For this reason it wanted to cut expenditure on armaments. The Chinese, perhaps half a century away from the time when they can produce non-essentials, could not bear to hear Krushchev hail communism as the way to a more pleasurable life. Life for them was still a grim struggle against poverty and starvation.

Krushchev carried on the quarrel energetically and with a great deal of publicity. When he fell from power in 1964, one of the charges against him was that he had turned the disagreement with China into a personal quarrel between himself and Mao. Nevertheless, the new Soviet leaders continued his policies. It was the Russians who, in 1966, called the Indian and Pakistani leaders to a conference in Tashkent to arrange for a withdrawal of their forces from the battle zones in Kashmir. In arranging this peace settlement, the Russians were obviously anxious to point out the contrast between their peaceful tactics and China's military aggression, and to suggest that Asian countries may find better friends in Moscow than in Peking.

The Soviet Union has herself quarrelled with China over the frontiers between the two countries. Most of the northern border of the province of Sinkiang is in dispute and there have been many accusations from each side that the other has illegally taken territory or persuaded large numbers of people to cross from one country to the other. Incidents like this were common during the long centuries before China and Russia became communist and help to remind us that the two nations have been enemies for most of their histories.

Hong Kong

The British colony of Hong Kong is made up of the island of that name and the town of Kowloon which were won by Britain in the Opium War. Added to the colony is a larger area of leased territory behind Kowloon. The lease was granted by the Manchus in 1898 and expires in 1998. Without this additional land Hong Kong could not possibly house her four million people, the great majority of whom are Chinese.

Despite the ease with which this could be done, the Chinese government has made no attempt to reclaim Hong Kong. At times she has encouraged riots and strikes by Chinese workers in the colony and made propaganda attacks on its British rulers. Yet food is still exported to Hong Kong and the Chinese were generous when drought threatened widespread famine there.

Obviously, one day, China will want Hong Kong back, but it is possible that she is waiting until 1998 when the lease runs out for the greater part of the area. Meanwhile Hong Kong is a useful centre for the transfer of foreign goods from ocean-going ships to coasting vessels which carry them to the

Ghurka soldiers guard the frontier between Hong Kong and China

ports of China. China is extremely active in building up her foreign trade, and profits from the fact that this collecting point is protected by Britain and would not, therefore, be attacked by one of Chiang Kai-shek's warships. The banking and shipping organizations of Hong Kong are also a useful way of making contact between China and the rest of the world.

23 Life in the New China

Chinese Women Today

One of the greatest blessings brought by the Communist government in China is the enormous improvement in the lives of Chinese women. In 1950 the Marriage Law forbade arranged marriages and gave women the same rights as their menfolk. Of course, merely passing a law was not enough; two thousand years in which women were little more than the slaves of their fathers and husbands could not be wiped out by the stroke of a pen.

It was not only the men who had doubts about the new law. Many women were too timid and too ill-educated to object when they were ill-treated in the old way. To tackle this problem, the All-China Women's Federation organized women's committees in every village and every street. Women cadres were sent to explain the new rights and to encourage women to demand equal treatment. Classes were started to teach women to read and write, as well as to explain the

Women soldiers

proper ways of caring for their homes and families. Women were also encouraged to attend political meetings, where the Communist Party's policies were explained, to give them the feeling that they could take part in building the new China.

They now play a very big part indeed. Nearly every Chinese woman works, leaving her young children at the nurseries provided by the communes and factories. They earn the same pay as men and are considered to be capable of doing any job. Many work on heavy jobs in the factories and drive tractors on farms. Some of them have important positions as managers in factories or leaders of work teams in the communes. Girls receive the same chance to study at university and college as boys, and many of them go on to be scientists, doctors and teachers.

Street Committees

Women usually play a leading part in the street committees that have been set up in every Chinese town. Before the Communists came to power, towns were notorious for their evil smelling alleys, without piped water, heaped with rubbish and black with flies. These have been cleaned up out of all recognition, thanks to the efforts of the street committees. Enthusiastic women have taken the lead in organizing their neighbours to remove rubbish, to paint their homes, to care for their children. They have co-operated in the countless campaigns that have been aimed at improving hygiene and health. In 1952, for instance, there was the drive against the 'five poisonous things'—mosquitoes, body lice, house-flies, rats and fleas. Posters and newspaper articles showed vividly the diseases that followed from these pests, and the street committees throughout China organized the people in their street to remove them. In campaigns such as this, a high sense of pride in their homes and neighbourhoods is built up and it becomes a thing of shame for a woman to neglect her home or show ignorance on questions of health.

Improvement in Health

By mass drives against the filth and vermin that bring disease, the Chinese have made their country the healthiest in Asia.

Women doctors at work in a public clinic

Epidemic diseases such as cholera, smallpox and typhoid no longer claim their thousands of victims each year. The most striking improvement of all is undoubtedly the fall in infant mortality. In 1949 nearly one hundred and forty out of every thousand children in Peking died before they reached the age of two. By 1956, the number had fallen to thirty-seven in every thousand, and since then it has been reduced in most areas to just over twenty per thousand, the same rate as in England.

This tremendous drive against ill-health and unnecessary death was begun at a time when China had only twenty thousand doctors trained in modern methods of medicine. On average this meant one doctor for every twenty-five thousand people. By 1960, the number of doctors had risen by five times, to one hundred thousand. This was a great improvement, but still not nearly enough, so, in medicine as well as steel making, 'walking on two legs' was necessary. Half a million doctors who practise the traditional Chinese methods of cure are allowed to work alongside the doctors trained in modern methods. Some of these traditional doctors rely on herbal cures and others practise acupuncture. These treat patients by pushing fine silver needles through the skin to stimulate nerve centres and relieve the tensions which cause pain. The old doctors can also be trained to carry out vaccinations, and to teach the people of remote areas about the importance of hygiene.

Education

It has been estimated that, in 1949, eighty per cent of the Chinese people were illiterate. Today that figure has been reduced to less than thirty per cent, most of whom are too old to begin to learn to read and write.

The mass drive for literacy began with adults. Classes were held in factories and in the villages, often by men and women who had never tried to teach before. They aimed at teaching all but the very old to read up to two thousand characters. With this elementary skill, men and women could read their daily newspapers and workers could follow written instructions.

The second stage was to make sure that all young children were taught in primary schools. To do this meant raising the number of places from about twenty million to a hundred million. Since 1962 compulsory primary education has been provided for all Chinese children. Now the Chinese are making every effort to see that all children can go on to secondary education for, without this, they cannot hope to bring about the advances in industry and science which their Five Year Plans have laid down. Still, only about one in every five children has a chance to go on to secondary education.

The key to the future lies in the hands of the university students. Between 1898, when the first Chinese university was opened, and 1949, not quite a quarter of a million students were trained by universities. In the first ten years after 1949, half a million students qualified, mostly as scientists, engineers, agricultural experts and doctors. The Communists have not yet the time, or the people, to spare for teaching many non-scientific subjects.

Every student learns from an early age that the purpose of education is to fit him or her to play a part in the future development of China. All schools and colleges expect their scholars to do manual work along with their other studies. Primary school children have gardens where they grow

Children in a primary school. The children with arm badges are also wearing the red scarves of the Young Communist organization, which it is a great privilege to join

vegetables, and they are taken out to help with the harvest. University students have to do two months' work each year in a factory, hospital or farm. Their professors, unless they are very old, have to do one month. In these ways the Communists hope that teachers and pupils will always remember that they are engaged in the struggle to raise living standards. This is emphasized in the long periods of political study, where students are taught the ideas of Karl Marx and trained to follow the leadership of the Communist Party. In England such indoctrination is thought very wrong. The Communists, however, believe that there is nothing wrong in teaching even the youngest children to have utter trust in their leaders. Only in this way, they think, will it be possible to continue progressing along the road to a communist society.

The New China

Most of the evils that Sun Yat-sen hated are now being eliminated in China. The women are free, the people healthy, the children able to read and write. The harsh power of the mandarin and landlord has been removed for ever. Modern science will soon fulfil Sun's dream of making China a great industrial nation and bring the benefits of the tractor, the aeroplane and the motor vehicle to all her people.

No longer are the Chinese despised and ill-treated in their own country. The notice in a Shanghai park which read, 'No dogs or Chinese allowed' has been torn down. China has become strong, too, outside her own borders. She is respected, and often feared by her neighbours in Asia and by the world's most powerful nations.

Of course there are many features of life in Communist China which we do not like, or cannot understand. Political propaganda among young children, brain-washing and one-party government, all seem wrong to people who live in countries where —very recently— ordinary people have become used to freedom. But these are also countries where the common man can enjoy, for the most part, a good standard of living and the benefits of social welfare. The Chinese Communists argue that there must be a period of party dictatorship to make the country strong enough to stand up to her enemies and to solve the problems of starvation and poverty. Nor should we forget that any Chinese over twenty-five was born into a country which was torn by war and suffering from the twenty years of corrupt government which had destroyed the chance that the dreams of Sun Yat-sen for a happier China might come true.

Further Reading

General

HILDA HOOKHAM, *A Short History of China*, Longman, 1969.

Making the Modern World series; 'Asia' by John Robottom and other authors, Longman, 1970.

MAURICE COLLIS, *Foreign Mud*, Faber, 1964 is a lively account of the opium trade.

Sun Yat-sen

ROBERT BRUCE, *Sun Yat-sen*, Oxford Clarendon biographies, 1969.

PEARL BUCK, *The Man who Changed China*, Methuen, 1955.

Mao Tse-tung

JEROME CH'EN, *Mao and the Chinese Revolution*, OUP, 1965 and

STUART SCHRAM, *Mao Tse-tung*, Pelican are the more detailed and accurate books.

ROBERT PAYNE, *Portrait of a Revolutionary*, N.Y., 1961 is a more colourful account of Mao.

China under the Kuomintang

JOHN GUNTHER, *Inside China*, contains some lively description of China in the 1930s.

The Communists

T. H. WHITE and A. JACOBY, *Thunder out of China*, London, 1947 and

H. FORMAN *Report from Red China*, N.Y., 1945 both tell the story of the war against Japan and the part played by the Communists.

R. C. NORTH, Chinese Communism, World University Library, 1966.

E. SNOW, *Red Star over China*.

TIBOR MENDE, *The Chinese Revolution*, London 1961.

C. P. FITZGERALD, *The Birth of Communist China*, Pelican 1964.

China since 1949

J. MYRDAL, *Report from a Chinese Village*, Pelican.

GUY WINT, *Common Sense about China*, Gollancz, 1960.

PING CHIA-KUO: CHINA, *The Modern World Series*, O.U.P.

There are many travellers' and journalists' accounts. Three of the most interesting are:

FELIX GREENE, *The Wall Has Two Sides*, Cape, 1963 (2nd Edn.).

BERYL GREY, *Through the Bamboo Curtain*, Collins, 1965.

D. CUSACK, *Chinese Women Speak*, Angus, 1958.

All these are more sympathetic to Communist China than the more difficult travellers' accounts.

The School of Oriental and African Studies, London University, issues a book-list for schools.

Index

Index

Index

Outline of Events

CHINA

MANCHU PERIOD (1644–1912)

1840–2	Opium War
1867	Sun Yat-sen born
1894	First rising by 'Dare-to-dies'
1896	Sun imprisoned in London
1911	The Double Tenth

YUAN SHI-KAI (President 1912–16)

1912	Manchu Emperor abdicates
1914	Japanese seize Shantung
1915	Twenty-one demands
1916	Death of Yuan

WAR-LORD PERIOD (1916–28)

1919	May Fourth Movement
1921	Chinese Communist Party founded
1925	Death of Sun
1926	Northern Expedition
1927	Shanghai Massacres
1928	Chiang Kai-shek enters Peking

KUOMINTANG PERIOD (1928–49)

1928–34	Kiangsi-Hunan Soviet
1931	Japanese seize Manchuria
1934–5	The Long March
1936	Sian Mutiny
1937–45	China at War with Japan
1945–9	Civil War between the Communists and Kuomintang

COMMUNIST CHINA (From 1949)

1950	Land Reform Law; Marriage Reform Law
1953–7	First Five Year Plan
1958	The 'Great Leap Forward'; Communes
1959	Rising in Tibet crushed
1960	Beginnings of quarrel with Russia
1964	China explodes nuclear bomb

THE WORLD

1884–5	China at war with France
1894–5	China at war with Japan
1901	Boxer Rebellion

1914–18	First World War

1917	Bolshevik Revolution in Russia
1919	Peace of Versailles
1924	Death of Lenin

1933	Hitler in power in Germany
1939–45	Second World War
1941	Pearl Harbour; America enters War

1950–3	Korean War
1954	Geneva Conference on Korea and Vietnam
1955	Bandung Conference
1962 and 1965	Chinese attacks on India